"The Bible clearly encourages Christians
surround themselves with godly friends a
states, we can only truly flourish with "an a
(Prov 11:14). Wise Guys is a careful and c... of the role
godly counselors play in the lives of Christians. For those who want to grow in maturity and wisdom, Evans' book deserves careful consideration."

— R. ALBERT MOHLER, JR.
President of the Southern Baptist Theological Seminary

"There is nothing more needed than practical resources to help men become what they were created to be. Wise Guys hits the nail on the head. Buy it and give it to every dude you know."

— DR. DARRIN PATRICK
Author of The Dude's Guide to Manhood and co-author of The Dude's Guide to Marriage

"Kent has written a remarkably clever, humorous, insightful and challenging book that is both readable and instructive. He recounts a host of personal examples accumulated over the years and concludes with 11 practical tips on how to be a better man, a more effective professional and more devoted disciple-maker. I predict you will thoroughly enjoy Wise Guys while you 'unlock hidden wisdom from the men around you.'"

— BOB RUSSELL
Retired Senior Minister, Southeast Christian Church

"This is a great read. Kent's practical, down-to-earth and intentional living is contagious. Now it's accessible in this book which will certainly shape how you think and live."

— DAN DUMAS
Author of Live Smart and Senior Vice President, The Southern Baptist Theological Seminary

"I've always defined true ministry as the process of walking through something with God and then being vulnerable enough to turn around and walk someone else through, too. Kent's infectious passion to develop Christ-like men is evident in his writing and you will be both challenged and inspired by this collection of characteristic profiles of men who have gone before to show the way. Bravo, Kent. You are walking us through."

— MARK HANCOCK
award-winning writer and Chief Executive Officer of Trail Life USA

"As men, we're so often attracted to the star of the podium, never considering the incredible people who worked so hard to get them there. But every single one of those medal-winners surrounded themselves with others who drew out strengths and train out the weaknesses. Using personal experiences with the ordinary men in his own life, Kent has written a candid and straightforward book that will encourage you to take an honest look at who you are and how you can get up and win as a husband, father and man."

— TIM SISARICH
Director & Host of Focus on the Family's Irreplaceable

"Kent doesn't just give us a list of qualities aimed at 'guilting' us to trying harder, to be better. Instead, he introduces us to a fist-full of men worth meeting. As the quick-to-read stories unfold, we get to know these wise guys. Thanks to Kent's honestly hilarious writing style, you'll drop your guard long enough to want to copy the character and wisdom generously offered in this book, man-to-man."

— DARREN WALTER
Lead Pastor, Current - A Christian Church

"In a creative and fresh way, Kent will set you on a journey of becoming a Wise Guy. His practical insight, honest evaluations, and life lessons will cause you to reflect on how you are engaging with others in your life. An easy read. I'd encourage any man to develop their own life lessons in the way Kent models."

— DR. DANN SPADER
President, Global Youth Initiative

"Kent has given us a roadmap for a new kind of organic mentoring – one that's perfect for those of us with little extra time to seek out formal mentoring relationships. He shows us how we as men can sharpen ourselves with the people we already do life with."

— TOM R. HARPER
CEO of Networld Media Group and author of Leading from the Lions' Den

"As you read this book, Kent Evans will take you on a journey. You'll learn what is required to become more the man God has called you to be. This book is going to get in your head and give you a brand new mindset."

— KYLE IDLEMAN
Teaching Pastor of Southeast Christian Church and Bestselling Author of Not a Fan

"Wise Guys focuses on who you can become as a godly man. It is full of wisdom you can use for every aspect of your life: as a father, husband, businessman or mentor. The examples and principles Kent develops are invaluable. It's easy to learn through the narratives of men who have 'been there.'"

— DAVE STONE
Senior Pastor of Southeast Christian Church

"I have come to appreciate Kent as a pragmatic, deep and balanced man. The wisdom in this book cuts across cultures and will speak to any man with ears to hear. It is a great resource for dads, and those of us who want to see a new generation of men who live out the three qualities David passed on to his son Solomon at his deathbed: be strong, act like a man and follow God (1 Kings 2). I highly recommend this book written by a great husband and dad."

— SIMON MBEVI
Executive Director of Transform Nations

FOREWORD BY BESTSELLING AUTHOR
KYLE IDLEMAN

Wise Guys

UNLOCKING HIDDEN WISDOM FROM THE MEN AROUND YOU

KENT EVANS
with Rob Suggs

Wise Guys: Unlocking Hidden Wisdom from the Men Around You

Published by City on a Hill Studio, LLC, Louisville, KY 40223

Editor: Lisa Griffin, Amy Simpson

Cover and Interior Design by Landon Brewer

ISBN 978-1-939622-28-0

Printed in the United States of America

For my beautiful wife April
who has patiently endured my growth
and loved me unconditionally
every step of the way.

CONTENTS

FOREWORD

I've been working on a list of things that are hard for me to say. Here's what I've got so far:

- I'm lost! Where can I ask for directions?
- Before I begin assembly, where are those instructions?
- I've had enough bacon.
- Sorry honey, I'm too tired. I just want to go to sleep.
- Hey bro, you want to run to the bathroom with me?
- Does this make me look fat?

The winner, though, might be this four-word golden great: "Will you help me?" I just tried to say that and nothing came out but a cough. Go ahead—try it yourself.

We guys are great at lots of stuff. I can throw that list together for you, too (Making lists actually is on that list!). But asking for help is not one of our primary skills. Which explains why we don't like to ask for directions or read the instructions. We're convinced we can do things ourselves. Doesn't matter what kind of skill we're talking about; we're on it, whether it's brain surgery or defusing a ticking bomb.

We want to be able to say, "Look! I operated on this brain

all on my own, and I never even went to med school!" Or, "Let's hear it for me—I just defused this b . . ."

There may be a few extra brain parts or bomb wires lying around afterward, but what matters to us is that we did it our way.

So we forge right into adulthood with our "I've got this!" flags flying. Looming ahead of us are marriage, fatherhood, career, and other crazy adventures. There are guys all around us who may not have read the directions at first either, but at some point they wised up. Some of them came from households with truly loving parents and terrific dads, and they have many of the answers we need.

We need to connect with those guys. We need to scrap the old DIY mentality, because being a husband, a father, a friend, and a devoted follower of Christ aren't the same as installing a new stereo system in your car. Some of this stuff goes boom.

On the manhood journey, we need help and we need each other, so you've come to the right place. As you read this book, Kent Evans, five-time world champion manhood ninja, will take you on a journey. You'll learn what is required to become more the man God has called you to be. And yes, I can hear some of you whispering the big question to each other: "Will there be—you know, lots of instructions?"

Hey, that's the best part! Yes, there will be some, but you

won't know it. Kent works his magic much like those dentists who use laughing gas. He may be pulling seven or eight of your teeth, but you won't really care. Kent's laughing gas is a collection of stories from his own "finding the directions" experiences. You're going to learn painlessly, and you're going to be laughing hard on certain pages. You'll also be on your way to becoming a manhood ninja just like Kent, and maybe without even losing any teeth. (Results vary.)

The real challenge of this book, however, isn't just to learn a series of lessons. It's to find yourself really wanting to find some men in your life who can walk with you, help you along, and move together toward the goal of being a real man of God. You're going to find yourself saying, "Yes, I've got some genuine questions about this issue and that one, but I can see that just makes me an ordinary guy. I also understand now that there are guys within reach who can help me get where I'm trying to go." And nothing could be more encouraging than that.

When it comes to being a top-rate, Grade-A, all-around stand-up guy in the current world, Kent's book is going to get in your head and give you a brand new mindset. Which isn't quite the same as brain surgery. I don't think.

Kyle Idleman

ACKNOWLEDGEMENTS

Let me share two points before you dive into this book.

1. WHERE ARE THE WOMEN?

This book is focused on men in my life who have provided me with advice, wisdom, and a life after which I have modeled my own. I've also learned from many women whom I admire—but no one in my adult life, man or woman, has impacted me more than my amazing wife, April. She is a faithful, godly, disciplined, and persistent woman who, by her daily example, is my best teacher and a constant source of inspiration.

My mom has also had an amazingly positive impact on my life. Nobody believes in me more. In fact, if she sees you reading this book, she will probably ask you why you didn't buy it sooner. She'll also shove more copies in your hands for all your friends. Then she'll snag a selfie.

But with women, my wife and mother are the extent of my close relationships. It's a high wall I've built. You won't read stories about other women who have shaped or molded me. Men have been my mentors. Still I should mention such women as my sisters, my steadfast mother-in-law, Carolyn Heisler, and friends like Doris Foster, Sandy Lawson, and Heather Bates, among many others. Without them, I'd be less the man than I am now.

2. APOLOGIES—BUT HANG TIGHT!

To my friends and mentors not included in this book, my apologies—but stay tuned. I've kept some of my powder dry. There's another book coming!

READ THIS FIRST

They tell me you don't read introductions.

After all, you're the reader, and editors have told me that readers skip introductions. They figure on going right to the good parts, and assume there are no good parts in introductions, prefaces, forewords, prologues, and preambles. And you've got a point. I'll admit to skipping a few in the past. I've noticed some of those things can be pretty boring when you're eager to get to the good parts.

But I think I have a few good parts in the next few pages, and I didn't want us to get off on the wrong foot when I started the introduction and found you weren't in your seat yet. That's why I went with "Read This First" instead. Now you'll be here for my Princess Bride line.

See, The Princess Bride is one of my favorite movies. It's a classic. If the title is unknown to you, then you and I are off to a poor start, my friend. However, I am willing to forgive. You can redeem our fledgling relationship (and do yourself a favor) by watching it soon.

That flick dumps a wheelbarrow full of top-notch comedy,

while delivering a boatload of great life lessons. Here is just one example: Never mess with a Sicilian when death is on the line. Crucial, I know. See, you have already snagged value from this book. You're welcome.

But here's a better one. In the course of the film, our hero Westley becomes stricken. His companions believe him to be dead. Their only hope is the legendary Miracle Max (Billy Crystal at his comedic finest). Against all odds, they cart him around for miles, finally spotting Max's ramshackle home in the woods. Westley's buddies drag him inside where the nutty wizard inspects the patient. He arrives at a diagnosis, declaring with raised eyebrows and a wagging index finger, "He is only mostly dead!"

We live in an age when another hero of ours is badly wounded and in need of miraculous resuscitation—not a physical hero, but a metaphorical one. I'm talking about mentorship. The good news: it's only mostly dead.

This hero has served mankind faithfully for thousands of years. He has performed amazing feats. He has fought for us, even swashbuckled. Far too few of us swashbuckle these days, if you ask me. Now our hero lies on the table of human history, limp and barely breathing.

Mentoring, the fabled method of learning from others more experienced, talented, or wise than ourselves, is mostly dead. And we are to blame, having nearly smothered him with our flippant indifference and staunch independence.

This is most acutely true among us men. We have lost the art of mentoring other men. More to the point, we have lost the art of being mentored ourselves.

We are individualistic to a fault. We esteem the "self-made man" (as if!) and talk of bootstrapping our way to success, going it alone. However, as John Donne famously declared, "No man is an island unto himself."

Even the Lone Ranger figured out he needed Tonto. We can learn from each other in ways that accelerate our success, help us avoid unnecessary suffering, and enhance our life experience.

THE HOME OF THE BRAVE

While this development is globally relevant, it's particularly true for Americans. There are many reasons why we're not mentoring in this country. We're all about self-reliance. No one tells us what to do, especially not a king or queen. We esteem the cowboy who needs no one and nothing to survive.

We are a relatively young nation that still vividly remembers the Boston Tea Party and the Declaration of Independence. Our political textbooks canonize men like

George Washington, Patrick Henry and Thomas Jefferson—fiercely independent men who, through the sheer strength of their will, galvanized this collection of independent states; men for whom I am grateful, but who, upon further inspection, were more community-based than the mythology we've built around them would suggest.

Additionally, our nation has enjoyed tremendous financial blessings—and a dose of the prideful spirit those blessings often bring. We laud the rags to riches innovator who eschewed all conventional wisdom, left his job (and maybe even his wife and children) to create the next amazing widget. We idolize individualism and praise the overgrown ego that often comes along with economic success.

We have geographic proximity but interpersonal isolationism. Some of our country's most successful individuals also became famously insular, paranoid, and even suicidal.

It wasn't always this way. Once upon a time we were better at learning from others. Not all that long ago, a young man learned as he walked behind his father who was plowing the back 40. He discovered not only how to cultivate, sow, and reap, but also learned about life, hard work, discipline, and overcoming adversity. He saw his own father and other men as wise, experienced individuals who were carriers of treasure in the form of wisdom—including the lesson of how to learn.

He learned by doing, observing, and asking. He questioned others about their experiences. He listened as they talked. Sure, he learned some things the hard way, but he also gleaned wisdom from those who went before him. He was brought up that way.

Why have we lost this capacity? Can we blame the disengaged youth? We find ourselves murmuring, "Those whippersnappers just don't care anymore. Earbuds in, always texting. These kids can't have a five-minute conversation with someone in the same room. They think they know everything—and what they don't yet know, they can Google!"

Surely, there's some truth in this. The folly of youth is often marked by an unwillingness to tap wiser minds, and this Information Age does put more data at our disposal than ever before.

However, to be honest, I believe we adults share more of the responsibility for this disconnect than we'd care to admit.

FATHERS HAVE ABDICATED

One key reason the mentor-protégé machine is broken: fatherhood has been obliterated in our country during the last 50 years. A father who stays married to one wife and gives guidance to his children is a relic, even the subject of scorn and ridicule.

Fatherhood is dying and this correlates directly to our unwillingness to learn from other men. More and more children are growing up in homes with, at best, a disengaged and selfish dad who brings home some of the bacon. At worst, they don't know their father at all. This is wreaking havoc on our society.

The fatherhood statistics are shocking, and they show no sign of heading back in the right direction. According to the National Fatherhood Initiative, the impacts of fatherlessness are far-reaching and extremely destructive: "There's a 'father factor' in nearly all of the social issues facing America today."

Their statistics indicate that children growing up in father-absent homes share the following disturbing traits:

- More likely to abuse drugs and go to prison
- Twice as likely to drop out of school
- Four times more likely to be poverty stricken
- Twice as likely to suffer obesity
- Seven times more likely to become pregnant as a teenager

Further, the organization reports that 24 million children in America are growing up in homes where the biological father is absent. That's one out of three!

Sure, many of these children have a loving stepfather in the picture, but that's not the norm. As a result of this tectonic paternal shift, we have moved from a "father knows best" paradigm to a mentality that defiantly declares, "Who in the heck is he to tell me anything?"

In fact, it's now become a badge of pride to grow up and make good without a father.

This was put into sharp focus by basketball superstar LeBron James. Mr. James has been fiercely devoted to his mother and routinely praises her. She gave birth to him when she was only sixteen years old. His father abandoned them and was never in the picture.

In February of 2014, Mr. James posted an open letter to his father, essentially thanking him for being gone. "Now, Dad, you know what, I don't know you, I have no idea who you are, but because of you is part of the reason who I am today [sic]. The fuel that I use—you not being there—it's part of the reason I grew up to become who I am . . . that maybe wouldn't have happened if I had two parents, two sisters, a dog, and a picket fence, you know?"

I have tremendous admiration for anyone who overcomes the lack of a father in his or her life. And I love the attitude that simply refuses to be a victim of circumstances. Mr. James could teach me a lot about hard work, self-discipline, and how to dunk like a boss! And, to his credit, he is heavily involved in programs like the Big Brothers and Big Sisters, doing his part to provide mentorship to those who otherwise might not have it. Hats off to him.

Even so, there's a danger in glorifying our own personal independence. It would be easy to take the words of Mr. James as an endorsement of fatherlessness as a motivational force. We can imagine some dad, pausing with a guilty conscience just before walking out on his family. Then he remembers what the basketball star said. "Maybe this will help my kids," he rationalizes, and he's gone.

Bad things happen when a father abdicates his responsibility. We socialize the perception that we can do whatever we want without anyone's help, especially that of a father.

This father-son schism cultivates a crop of young men who have hardly ever turned to an older man and learned anything at all. Or maybe they did learn a lesson or two: how to be selfish, abusive, or just plain absent.

What happens when a young man grows up and thinks he needs no father? It's not a great reach from there to the conclusion that he doesn't need to be one, either.

And the cycle continues.

REVERSING THE TREND

With this sad social course in mind, I share my story.

Actually, I share a whole connected series of them. These are narratives of men who have poured into me along my life's journey; men whose counsel I sought and continue to seek.

These are tales you might find interesting and perhaps even relatable. However, having you understand my story is not the aim of this book.

If you simply comprehend my situation, then you will have missed the point. If you pick up a few tips from the stories in this book, you will have caught half the point. But, if as you read, you consider people in your own life whom you could humbly approach for help, then you have caught the entire point.

My aim: to help men once more learn how to learn from each other. I want the fatherless teenager to realize there are thousands of men out there who can help him, if only he could find the courage to ask. Our society would benefit if we shifted our male maturity paradigm from fiercely independent to aggressively interdependent. And I want the current father to see that he's not alone on his journey, either.

Let's spark a revolution that changes how men relate to each other! Let's become a truly multigenerational, arm-linked society of men who help each other grow, learn, and succeed.

TRUE STORIES

Rather than suggest you should go and do this, I will show

you how I went and did this. I'll do that through 16 personal stories. They involve key men whom God placed in my life, often at crucial junctures when I was ready to listen. They have shaped who I have become.

Some of these stories involve men with whom I am close friends and I connect on a regular basis. Some describe one-time encounters so profound I never forgot the engagement. Some of these men knew I was trying to learn from them. Some were unaware, just living their life in a way that was worth modeling.

Perhaps most importantly, all of these men are regular guys I've met through the course of my life. Friends, bosses, colleagues, and co-volunteers. I did not need to be a powerful politician, evening news anchor, or famous celebrity to gain access to these men. They were available to a regular guy like me. Like you.

The first few stories are sequential. They illustrate how my journey began, and they highlight the impact of key early participants who gave me needed tools to continue growing and learning. Beyond that, the stories are not presented in any specific order. Each man gave me a new tool that I tossed into my interpersonal toolbox. The order in which I threw them in there is not materially significant.

Let's start by focusing on where my journey began: in a nondescript office in my hometown of Louisville, Kentucky.

FIGURE YOURSELF OUT

Beware the Un-something!

I was 17 when he said it, but it might as well have happened five minutes ago. His voice still reverberates in my ears nearly three decades later. "Kent, you cannot become the Un-something." Huh? Did I hear him right? What exactly is an "un-something"? That's a Dr. Seuss character, right?

He went on to explain. And with that one statement, this man released shockwaves of change into the fabric of my life. His sage advice set me on a radically different path. It has paid amazing dividends in all that I've done.

Allow me to tell you how I came to be in this man's office and to come face to face with the dreaded Un-something.

In my late teen years, my parents went through a divorce. As a teenager, I didn't quite know what to do with all the emotions surrounding this development. My mother worked for a company that offered free counseling to her family members. When it became obvious I could use a little help, I was assigned a kind and insightful family therapist, Weldon C. Fuller.

You know those old Humphrey Bogart movies that feature a detective with his name emblazoned on the frosted glass door? That's how I remember Weldon's office. I may have romanticized it a bit, but I'm sticking with that version. At least I haven't started to recall it in black and white, with smoke wafting from a nearby receptionist who is holding a cigarette in that long stick thingy, so I've got that going for me. Regardless, I can still see his name emblazoned on the door, complete with the middle initial.

In our sessions, as any good counselor does, he asked lots of questions. I answered them as best I could. One thing I did not suffer from was suppressing my thoughts and feelings. I was afflicted with the opposite disease: I was a blabbermouth (a verbal condition I've yet to overcome, if you ask certain people).

As we met, I unloaded. After a few sessions, I became quite comfortable with this skilled listener. In our third session together, he had taken in my story, and it was time to provide some gentle steering and guidance. He pointed out how focused I was on my father and his role in the divorce. This is what he was hearing from me: "I won't end up in the same situation they're in!"

So Weldon gently said, "You know, Kent, life has a peculiar way of turning you into the very thing you don't want to become. Put another way, psychologically speaking, you cannot become the 'Un-something.'"

He allowed that life-changer to sink in for a second, then he continued: "You'd rather not end up in this same situation? Fine, I get it. But my advice to you is this: Stop trying to not do this or not be that. Instead, find some men who have the life you want, and figure out why their situation is the way it is. Then do some thinking. What is it that makes these guys worth imitating? What do they have or embody that you want? Learn from them and then model yourself after the parts you like."

I had no idea how significantly his words would affect my life. Perhaps I still don't fully grasp the total impact. He had reached into my cerebral cortex, yanked out a fistful of wires, and reconnected them in a new scheme. A mental rewiring in five words! You cannot become the Un-something. This guy was good.

Can you relate to this story? Did you have trouble as a young person, and a kind helper gave you the tools you needed to overcome your situation?

Or, more to the core of the issue, did you ever say to yourself, "I won't become like _____________!" And, for maybe five, 10, or 30 years, you lived in a vortex of avoidance, desperately trying to evade a destination, when you didn't even know where your ship was headed in the first place?

I suspect that on some level, many men can relate to my story. There are a few reasons I believe this.

TARGET UNKNOWN

I think most people (men in particular) struggle to clearly articulate a vision for their desired mature state. Said another way, most of us don't know who we want to be when we grow up.

Let's use a short quiz to figure out if you are the exception to this general rule.

Grab a sheet of paper. And about that: You can do this thing in your mind, but it's much more effective in writing (decoder: more effective = more painful).

At the top of the sheet, write, "Who I want to be in five years." Then, below that, write down a half dozen character traits you would like to embody five years from now. Avoid positional goals such as "get married" or "become vice president." We're looking for character traits you'd like to manifest, or skills you'd like to have.

I know what you're thinking. I can almost see the glazed look in your eyes. Yes, I could provide examples to help you get started, but that would kind of defeat the purpose, now wouldn't it?

Most of us wouldn't do well on this quiz. Why? Because we have no clue. We've spent zero time thinking about it. But just in case you're one of the intentional ones who just aced this part of the chapter (The List)—you're not done yet. Here comes Part Two (The Pursuit).

Below, or next to each of the traits, write down what you're doing to embody that trait or develop that skill in your life. Clarification: Not what you should be doing or might start doing someday—what you're actually, physically, real-time, officially doing at the present. As in, now. What active steps are you taking to intentionally turn you into the man you want to be?

If you completed Parts One and Two without Googling something, congratulations! You are way ahead of the curve. In fact, I'll tell you what. Send me your list through social media (@manhoodjourney) and I will send you something valuable. I'm not precisely sure what that might be yet—I'm not exactly stocking up—but it will be amazing! I promise.

Men, we don't see the target! We are shooting blind—if

we have any bullets at all. And even for the few who have a target in the crosshairs, most of us have no clue where we are relative to it. Are we near it already? Are we inching closer to it, or drifting farther from it? Are we cruising at high speed, or crawling at a snail's pace?

What's our vector, Victor?

CAREER FOCUS

There's another issue. Sometimes we may have a couple of goals, but they're enmeshed with our role at work. We have replaced personal identity with career aspiration. We no longer know who we want to be; we only know what we want to do.

Allowing our identity to be driven by our careers is a dangerous game. Why? That identity is not always fully within our control. It can be stolen from us by a vindictive boss, unpredictable market forces or a new parent company that just needs to go in "another direction." For anyone who has suffered the unpredictable loss of a job, it's a major gut check.

I've been fired twice (I'll man up and admit I clearly deserved one of those boots). Placing our personal identity into our chosen line of work is like leaning back in a chair. We look cool right up to the moment someone kicks the legs out from under us.

If you're like most men, when you think of who you are, you don't have a person in mind; you have a role. We need to be absolutely sure we're making this distinction, because this distinction will be the making of us.

Men, don't trade down. Our identities are too often summarized in our job title, or fully outlined within our curriculum vitae. We are who LinkedIn says we are. Talk about identity theft! When this one gets snatched, some men never find it again.

EGOTISTIC INDIVIDUALISM (A.K.A.: THE POT TALKS TO THE KETTLE)

On to the final round.

This may be the best indicator of all, but fair warning: it might hurt a little. It hurts me even to write it.

This one comes in the form of a question:

When is the last time you observed another man's expertise and asked him to help you with that skill?

If you can recall a singular recent example, bully for you. You are the exception to the rule!

Let's say you have a neighbor with a perfectly manicured lawn. Mine is Dan (the guy is retired, so there's your explanation, or most of it anyway). You ogle this fellow's lawn jealously, with your feet planted squarely amidst the crabgrass and bare spots in your own. You know what they say about "the grass is always greener." In this case—well, it just is. You figure it's time to upgrade the premises.

So, what do you do? Well, if you have some money (and brains), you hire professionals. If you're on too tight a budget, you scour YouTube for videos on power seeding in the fall (men love YouTube videos: anonymous advice seeking, what a concept!).

Those tactics may work, but why not try something radical? Go knock on Dan's door and ask him for some help.

It goes like this:

"Dan, your lawn is amazing. I'm, well, green with envy. Got any tips?"

If we were all in a big room reading this book at the same time, right now, it would resemble one of those chaotic British Parliament sessions we see on the news. Just suggesting this approach would have guys hollering and throwing their wigs at me. You know it and I know it.

Why do we hate this suggestion so vehemently? Ego. That's the reason.

We see men in our lives every day who are better than we are at something. They have more financial success, leadership experience, marital bliss, fatherly wisdom, or bow tie tying skill. We don't actively learn from them because we have been conditioned not to. There's a show to put on, right? If we ask for someone's help, we take off the mask and reveal to the world that we're weak (as if there were any doubt, considering we're members of the human race). It's pride, plain and simple, and it manifests itself in two ways.

The first problem comes when our egos blind us from even recognizing these men and their accomplishments. We're so wrapped up in proving ourselves to the world that we don't take the time to observe the proficiency of others. We drive right by the amazing lawn, never noticing the perfectly trimmed edges. As if by just observing their proficiency we are somehow admitting our own uselessness.

Second, our ego tells us that once we've recognized their proficiency, the game is on! It's not a teachable moment—it's a battle. We have to catch up, and preferably, we'll pass them while they're sleeping so we can greet them at the self-built finish line with an arrogant smirk. We're on a personal quest to be better than almost everyone at virtually everything. The world is one big king-of-the-hill tussle, and that's pretty exhausting.

This is where my journey began. In Weldon's office. That's the place where I first learned to lift my eyes, observe the men at the crest of the hill and reach for a hand up. It's there I began a lifelong pursuit of learning from the wisdom of others. At the end of the book, in the tradition of Paul Harvey, I will tell you "the rest of the story" regarding Weldon.

But for now, let's turn our attention to the many men who have directly affected who I am today. They have poured into my life over breakfasts, lunches, and countless phone calls and cups of coffee (You're welcome, Starbucks).

They're my mentors and role models. I've enshrined them in my personal hall of fame. They've shown me something to aspire to, so that I don't chase the unattainable un-something.

For each man, I've listed a few lessons learned. In most cases this grossly undervalues their contributions. But I've chosen the lessons I believe will resonate with you as you read this book. Most of all, they might point you toward the mentors just on the outskirts of your life—men waiting to help your transformation to the person you're on your way to becoming.

2

ENCOURAGE RELENTLESSLY

Be Grateful—Then Do Something About It

ith the exception of my amazing wife, my best friend in life is Dave Hare. He and I met as young boys, and it's a good thing we got along so well. We tended to be in the same places at the same times.

Our families lived in the same neighborhood and enrolled in the same sports programs. Dave and I attended the same kindergarten, in the Presbyterian church on top of the hill near Dave's home at the time.

They say if you make it through life with one true and absolute friend, you should consider yourself blessed. In my case, I do. Dave has always been that go-to guy for me--not that we're able to hang out as much as we could when we were younger. The pace of our lives keeps us a little too preoccupied, but we try not to let a month get by us without making some kind of connection. It might be lunch or just a quick phone chat, but somehow, someway, we're going to link up. I think you'd like Dave, because I can't imagine anyone who wouldn't.

Of course it's also true that Dave is the guy who holds the secrets, when it comes to my past deeds and misdeeds. Other than my wife, nobody else is in a better position to bring about my public humiliation. He alone holds the key to a mental repository of incriminating Kentformation.

But I'm not worried. Dave is such a kind soul you'd probably have to apply torture to get the relevant facts out of him. He knows all about the vehicles I've crashed, the Little League property I've defaced, the cans of Grape Crush I've detonated in anger—hey, enough about that stuff. The point is, Dave has seen it all when it comes to my life: the good, the bad, and the extremely ugly. We've hit the usual high points and low points of life together. Maybe you have a friend like that.

When I think about Dave's accomplishments, there's one that stands out, as far as I'm concerned. In our 40-year friendship, his crowning achievement was strictly accidental. He didn't know it at the time, but when we were in our early 20s, he indirectly convinced my wife to marry me.

April and I had been dating for some time, and she noticed

how many times I mentioned this Dave character. It was clear he was a big part of my life, and finally she had the chance to meet him. Dave and I were umpiring baseball games, and one night, after the game, she and Dave were able to spend some time together and make an acquaintance. My best friend won April's seal of approval, and she made the leap to the conclusion that I just might make a good husband.

How? Her reasoning was that any guy who had a friend like Dave carried some strong credentials. It stood to reason that any guy with a friend like him must be a decent guy himself. I owed Dave my life—and my wife!

HOUSE OF DAVE

Now you couldn't have seen where I was going with this, but...this chapter isn't about Dave. But I haven't been wasting your time. You needed a few basic facts about my friend and his importance in my life in order to appreciate what the chapter is about, which is the home Dave came from.

When we were kids, Dave's family attended church. As a matter of fact, the word attended probably doesn't cover it. They dwelt in church; they were church-dwellers rather than merely churchgoers. None of this "live one way the rest of the week, then act Christian on Sunday" stuff for them. They were genuine and real. And at the same time, they were never dull and pious. Dave had some crazy older brothers, for one thing.

But it was a very nice place for a kid to visit. I loved the Hares and spent quite a bit of time at their residence with Dave. When I was there, I felt comfortable and able to be myself. It was an open and loving environment, and I knew there was something unique about it. But I didn't connect the dots until I was away at college and received the letter.

You've just read about how Weldon, my counselor, had encouraged me not to become an un-something, but to find traits of people I truly admired, and be conscious about pushing toward those attributes in my own life. By this time, when I was in college, I was trying to follow his advice. I kept a running mental list of men I knew who seemed to have it all together—or at the very least who had something in their lives I didn't. My list had names and the traits that went with those names. And atop that list stood the name of John Hare, my best friend's dad.

I would have put John Hare in the "has it all together" list. As far as I could tell, he was the prototypical suburban father, "Ward Cleaver" in an age when Ward Cleaver was no longer in style. He loved his wife, Ginnie, faithfully until she succumbed to Alzheimer's in 2004. He sang in the church choir and even took his musical talents on the road quite often to help out at revivals or potluck picnics. He coached baseball where Dave and I spent all our waking summer hours.

He carried off the whole husband-and-dad thing while being, to all appearances, just an ordinary guy. He had (and has) one of those laughs that captures a room, travels down the hall, and recruits people to share in it. You'd find yourself laughing along uproariously, yet thinking, They may have to call the paramedics. This guy's about to combust! He was the only guy I've ever known who laughed with heart, soul, mind, and strength. And how infectious is that?

When I think back to those times, I remember a man who was pretty much happy all the time, who found lots to laugh about. There was an effervescence about him, an infectious zest for life. It was a simple, engaging manner, containing within it a depth and a sense of peace that comes only when someone is attentive to where he is and whom he's with. While I couldn't have labeled it during my teen years, the time came when I found a name for the trait he had. It was joy. And I suppose it's not surprising that joy traveled to the very top of my list. What could be worth more in life?

THE LETTER

John, I thought, I want your joy.

Interestingly, I did not have to pick up the phone and call John to ask him where to shop for that brand of joy. God took care of that little detail. Then he nudged John to show me how to use it.

Somehow John understood that I could use a little encouragement. One day while I was in college, I received a letter. I was pleased to hold in my hands a three-page letter in John's handwriting. But I was just as curious to know why this unsolicited letter had arrived in my post office box.

I read over the epistle a couple of times and saw that it had two main points. First, John wanted to thank me for being his son's friend. How many dads ever write that letter or verbalize that gratitude? Dave's dad did.

Second, there was a friendly suggestion. John felt it would be a good idea for me to look into the idea of God—who he was and how much he loved me. I think he knew me well enough by that time to understand that I would receive these words well. It was just the right time in my life, and I was open to what he was suggesting.

But for me, the significance of the letter was in the fact that he had sent it in the first place. I suppose that in his talking about how much God cared, I saw how much he cared. Also, probably without realizing it consciously, I did tentatively begin to connect two dots: John had joy. John had a relationship with God. Hmmm.

I sat and looked at the letter, torn open in my hand, filled with a busy man's handwriting. Nobody had required him to write to me, as far as I knew. He took the time to thank me for being his son's friend. In that moment, I didn't just want the joy—I wanted to be a dad, because that's what this man was. I wanted to have a son who had a friend, and then I wanted to write a letter just like this one to that son's friend. Not only did I have a trait list; I had added an item to my bucket list. Write a letter this cool to your son's buddies.

I'd never thought about the future this way, never had an aspiration like this that had to do simply with being a good person.

And lest we forget, this letter was sent in the last millennium, a dark and scary era some of us refer to as BF (Before Facebook). Back then, getting a message to someone actually involved physical effort. You couldn't just direct-message them on Twitter or tap out a quick text message. The shortcuts weren't there. You needed ink, paper, an envelope, and even an external light source. You looked up their address in a ten-pound phone book. Your quest also required a magical device called a postage stamp, which cost you real cash money.

The combination of a few elements dramatically heightened this letter's impact on me.

First, it was the heart behind it—gratitude.

Second, it was unsolicited, demonstrating love and care for me.

Third, I had yet to begin my journey of finding men I wanted to be like. But this incident pushed me in the right direction. It felt like a small miracle.

Given all this, I sat in my dorm room and read the letter intently. No, I drank that letter. It was like water to a thirsty man stranded in his own desert of cluelessness. I would use words like savored and cherished. Given that I'm telling you about it now, you can see the impact one man made with a pen and three sheets of stationery.

LESSONS LEARNED

What life lessons can we harvest from John Hare and his letter?

First, John showed me an act of kindness. He taught me to be others-focused. Here was a "real man," a family leader, a joyful dad who found it worthy of his time to do something completely unselfish.

Second, he helped me begin to open my heart to a loving father who I knew about but didn't really know. More to come on that one, but you get the idea.

Third, he demonstrated that a letter can be a great way to encourage and even challenge someone, when written in love.

Fourth, he gave me a foreshadowing of a father's love for the friends of his children—a healthy outlook for a possible future. He taught me to care about those who mean something to those I love.

Finally, he taught me to continue being a father even after my children leave home.

John Hare unknowingly lowered the cornerstone into place for the new life I was building. His letter was the first piece of a puzzle. And the best part was that I had not tried to find it. It found me.

Questions to Consider

- *Who in your life needs some encouragement?*

- *Who is your child's or wife's best friend?*

- *Have you ever expressed gratitude for that person's contribution to a life that is precious to you?*

- *Would this person more appreciate a Facebook post they can share with their friends? Or would they like an old-school letter written with ink on paper?*

There's no time like the present, which is a word meaning: write now!

3

ALWAYS BE ASKING

Ask the Right Questions. Unlock the Right Doors.

How many of us can say we had a boss who genuinely cared for us? A supervisor who understood his role as developing us rather than simply using us toward company goals? A manager so confident and assured in his own role that he could freely pour his own accumulated wisdom into us?

I've been blessed with a number of great mentors in my career. None had more significant impact than Frank Austin. His impact on me would be impossible to measure. Sure, he taught me practical lessons about sales, business management, and working well with others. But the real treasures were his lessons in the skill of all skills: the fine art of expanding my influence. The things I learned from him have served me every day of my life since then.

I met Frank at a pivotal point in time, to say the least. I was unemployed and desperate to find work. To make matters more interesting, I'd been married less than 18 months and fired from two different jobs in a span of less than 90 days. You read that correctly: two jobs. Both had unraveled quicker than you can say, "Where do I file for unemployment?" My finances were in shambles. Debt was mounting. My supportive but quizzical wife was wondering how I would get us back on track.

I needed a lifeline, and not just financially. I was a smart young man, but I had a lot of growing up to do. Intelligence was not the issue; maturity was.

All I knew was that I wanted a job. But in God's mercy and grace, he gave me so much more. I received a caring mentor and friend, a lifeline. Then, along with all of this, God threw an income into the deal for good measure.

It's not inconsequential that these blessings were given at the perfect moment—a time when I was ready to learn, listen, and begin to change. Finding Frank at that moment in my life would be like landing on the Appalachian Trail and stumbling across Davy Crockett. So, you know your way around these here woods, eh?

Frank's influence on me was remarkable--the way we met, even more so.

Since I was unemployed, my brother-in-law Troy kindly let me pick up some hours with his electrician crew during the summer. I had no electrical skill, but I could hammer stuff, carry random objects, and generally follow directions. While riding in his truck one day, he took a call from a customer whose voice I overheard on Troy's in-car speaker cell phone—an exotic item that was way ahead of its time.

I listened to this conversation, then turned to my brother-in-law and asked about the caller. Troy relayed his name and then added, "You ought to see this guy's brand new house. I did when we were wiring it. Quite a place."

I did some quick math in my head: amazing new house = successful guy. My job-seeking antennae were up all the time in those days.

"Troy, out of curiosity, what does this guy do for a living? Do you happen to know?"

"I think he's a sales and marketing exec. Why?"

Troy probably saw my eyes go widescreen. I had a degree in marketing! "Call him back," I stammered. "Right now!"

You can figure out the rest. To summarize, the best business mentor of my life appeared because I happened to be sitting in the right truck with the right in-law electrician on the right day at the right moment. I could have labored feverishly for weeks or months on my own without hitting this particular winning lottery number. Go figure.

Depending on your philosophical orientation, you could call it random chance, rabbit's-foot luck, or universal karma. Me, I call it a personal gift from a loving heavenly father. And it's the kind of thing that tends to happen when the student is well-prepared (read: twice-humbled). In that situation, the teacher tends to appear with the lesson.

I met Frank for lunch, and to cut to the chase, after a few conversations, I landed a job on his team. That was another miracle. He just so happened to have role in mind for which I was a solid fit. During this turning point season of my professional life, I soaked in Frank's leadership and teaching for three years. These days I'm still on the receiving end, but it tends to come through the occasional phone call or breakfast at Frank's early morning dive of choice, the local Bob Evans restaurant.

Frank is difficult to describe in a few words. When we met, he was an accomplished businessman with a few decades of sales success and senior leadership under his belt. Not only could he ink the deals—lots of guys can do that—he could teach others how to ink the deals. In the business world, if you find someone like that, you have the goose who laid the golden egg. He can churn out copies of himself. And in my case, he was willing to do it with a guy who was still carrying two pink slips in his vest pocket; a guy with a lot of want-to but not too much has-done.

Due to his success and vision, Frank had been asked to revitalize a business division. He allowed me to play a key role in that project for several years.

Of the many things Frank taught me, I will focus on the most impactful one: He taught me how to ask great questions.

You may be thinking, "That's it? How to ask great questions? Why should I care?"

Hey, you just did it! Good job. And it's my pleasure to offer a great answer to your great question. Would you mind if I do it by way of analogy?

You and I can both throw a ball. Also, Mariano Rivera. He can throw a ball, too. The difference between him and us is a couple hundred million in the bank, international stardom, and a guaranteed spot in the Baseball Hall of Fame.

So throwing a ball may be ordinary, but there are championship levels of doing ordinary things. Frank is the Mariano Rivera of question-asking. And, just to overwork the analogy: Mariano closed baseball games, Frank closed new sales deals. After three years under his major league tutelage, I could hold my own in the Q&A game too.

Perfecting the art of asking great questions is like finding the master key to many of life's doors.

Armed with superior interrogative skill, almost nothing

you want to learn or accomplish is beyond your reach.

This is the reason I put Frank Austin's chapter so early in this book. His impact was akin to the first step in a nuclear reaction. It set off everything else. He gave me the tool I would need to learn not only from him but from anyone.

While volumes can be written on this topic, let's explore a few high level benefits of becoming great at asking questions.

UNLOCKING THE NEEDS OF OTHERS

Frank was always looking for ways he could add value, professionally and personally. He clung to one simple truth: that if he wanted to help someone, he had to clearly understand what they needed. So simple, yet so overlooked.

He'd say, "Kent, customers only buy for one of two reasons. Either they're experiencing a pain that they believe your product can alleviate. Or they believe your product can give them a pleasure they're yet to enjoy." He was always probing for those pain or pleasure points with everyone—bosses, colleagues, vendors and prospective customers.

He was assertive, not pushy. He would back out of a deal if it was not a fit for the customer. If he determined his products did not align with their needs, he would admit that and move on. But, as he asked questions, if he learned that he could meet their needs, he dove in and explained his solution. People trusted and respected Frank not because he was a schmoozer, but because he was honest and genuinely interested in their well-being.

We're usually so consumed with our own needs and issues that we don't stop to learn those of others. When asking questions, we're shelving our own issues for a moment and seeing the world from someone else's perspective. Like a caring and intelligent doctor first diagnoses before suggesting a remedy, we should adopt a similar posture.

This isn't a business thing; this is a life thing. Unless you live by yourself on a tiny little island, this concept applies again and again. What does your spouse need? Your children? Your parents? Your boss? Your pastor or priest?

If you don't know, or you're fuzzy on the concept, it means you haven't asked and listened. Start asking great questions.

EXTENDING OUR INFLUENCE

It's cliché, but it's true: People don't care how much you know until they know how much you care.

If you want to have influence, you have to learn how to care—truly care, not pretend-care—about the interests of others. Frank used a terrific metaphor to help me understand this.

"I'm just a guy on one side of a pond," he said. "There's someone over on the other side whom I need to convince to join me on this side. Soon after, we may or may not say that person is on our side of the pond. Let's say it has dozens of lily pads floating on top. The first thing I have to do is figure out, through artful, intentional, and sequential questioning, where this other person is located. Is she on the far side, anchoring herself to a tree with her arms folded? Is she standing on a lily pad in the water—or is she as close as the one in front of me, only one step from my shore?"

Knowing the customer's present location was essential to determining whether Frank could add value. This seems obvious. But, it was the step most often ignored by Frank's competitors. He turned that to his own advantage. Most salespeople want to talk; Frank wanted to listen.

You may not be a salesperson, so you wonder if this analogy applies to you. Well, have you ever wanted to influence another human being—maybe your spouse, adult child, employee, or even the waiter at your favorite restaurant? Gaining influence requires earning the right to be heard: gaining credibility by demonstrating a true connection. We often discover there are fewer "lily pads" between us than we thought.

Frank would use questioning like a surgeon uses a scalpel.

He sought to heal and serve, not to harm or manipulate. You would notice pretty quickly that he uses one phrase repeatedly: "Help me understand." Our favorite phrases speak to who we are, and his own painted a picture of someone who wanted to know more about everyone he was with. His catch phrase was legendary on our team. He taught me how to be inquisitively assertive and to harvest information from others in a way that was helpful to them and productive for me.

LESSONS LEARNED

Perfecting the art of asking great questions unlocks our power of influence. When we seek to understand, we are in a relationally humble and winsome position. It can improve our marriage, enrich our relationship with our kids and accelerate our careers. Here are a few of the lessons we can learn.

First, questions position the other person as a helper. It's human nature to help those in need. When we ask questions, especially any that begin with the words "help me" or "can you," we tap into a person's inner sense of duty and assistance. It normally opens doors and keeps defenses down.

Second, we position ourselves as curious learners. One thing that is true about the vast majority of people we know: They'd rather talk about themselves than talk about us. So when we ask questions and listen to their answers, we are allowing them to enjoy their favorite activity.

Third, asking questions is only part of the process. Frank often said, "Listening to someone is paying them the supreme compliment in life." When we ask meaningful questions and listen intently, we are giving the other person the place of honor.

Jesus was the greatest question asker. Instead of always preaching, he was most frequently asking questions – questions that launched adventures in self-discovery and healing.

That's what I want to do, and I'm sure you do as well. My goal is more than selling—it's to create true connections with people in order to make this life into something better. The adventure of a lifetime begins with one great question.

Questions to Consider

- *On a scale of 1-10, how would you rate yourself as a questioner? What would you need to change to move up the scale one notch?*

- *Would those who know you describe you as more of an asker or a talker?*

- *When you get around accomplished people, do you try to impress them or learn from them?*

- *When is the last time you asked a loved one—maybe your spouse or children—three questions in a row without interjecting your opinion of their answers?*

- *When you ask questions, do you listen with the intent to respond or the desire to understand?*

- *Are you having relational or work conflict with someone? Have you asked them to help you fully understand their perspective?*

4

CORRECT GENTLY

Your Blood Pressure (and Theirs) will Thank You.

I thought about asking you to skip this chapter. I knew I needed to write it down in full honesty, but I didn't really want you to read it. But if I placed a note at the beginning that said, "Move along, nothing to see here," maybe I could still call this a frank and honest book without utterly humiliating myself.

So, considering that what follows is highly embarrassing, if I asked you simply to skip ahead to Chapter 5, would you be kind enough to do so? I didn't think so. Thanks a lot, buddy.

I made this little mistake so that you don't have to, so walk with me to the Kent Evans Hall of Shame, 11th floor. (I know, it's a big place, and still under construction, unfortunately).

For several years I earned my living as a small business owner. I liked to call myself a "marketing mutt" who tackled all sorts of communication projects for business clientele. One week I'd be working on a brochure for a catering firm; the next, writing a marketing plan for an energy consultant; the next, building a website for a general contractor. What I couldn't handle, I'd subcontract and mark up.

I didn't earn the big bucks, but those few years were enjoyable, all in all. Wearing so many hats, I often found myself in the midst of moments that taught me a lot about myself—where I was competent, and where it turned out I'd had delusions of adequacy.

One of those moments occurred while working on a project for a local roofing company. It was led by a reputable and talented CEO, Rick Steinrock. Rick's team did high end work and I considered it a privilege to work directly with him on a new website for his company. The same qualities you wanted in your roof, he personally embodied: he was reliable, sound, and dependable. That was probably why customers trusted him and employees were loyal to him.

Rick was, in many ways, a typical small business owner. He was direct and commanded attention among his team and peers. He could smoothly transition from discussing options with a customer to giving direct instructions to a team of roofers to negotiating costs for materials from a supplier. His experience had provided him with a full toolbox of skills needed to be successful in the competitive and not-always-above-board construction industry.

There was another side to Rick: With all this high confidence and utter competence, he was humble and easy to work with. The stereotype of someone in his kind of work would be that he'd be the gruff and demanding alpha dog. Instead, he was calm, unassuming and self-controlled.

Not that he was a pushover. He personified the fully masculine man described in Aubrey Andelin's excellent book, The Man of Steel and Velvet. He could deliver a solid punch—softly. It may not be possible in boxing, but it can be done as a communication skill. He could wound with the intent to heal. Allow me to share the circumstances that led me to receive one of these velvety smooth blows to the gut.

As a man of high character and integrity, Rick expected full accountability from those with whom he worked. His word was his bond, and if you engaged with him, He expected the same from you. At this point in my career, I was more talented than I was dependable. I had a nasty habit of overcommitting myself and then allowing projects to flounder.

While working on the website for Rick, I became overloaded. I had made too many commitments to too many clients, and I fell way behind on deadlines. I don't recall intentionally pushing Rick's project to the bottom of my list, but for whatever reason, I allowed it to suffer the most. When some deadlines were missed, I began receiving calls from Rick asking for updates. I compounded the problem of being behind by trying to dodge Rick's calls, and I failed to return a few of them. I'm giving you something worth more than gold here—don't make this basic mistake. If you're trying to avoid someone, don't attend the same church that he does. As Muhammad Ali said: you can run but you cannot hide. And remember, he had quite a punch.

When compiling your list of people to avoid, it's wise to start with people you're unlikely to run into. At least one major ocean between the two of you is a good rule of thumb. The Pacific is a nice choice. You're welcome.

But as I said, I did this so you won't have to. One day, as I exited our church sanctuary, I spotted Rick in the hallway. Before I could duck behind a trash can, he spotted me. It had been about three weeks and a few unreturned phone calls since we talked. Rick calmly headed toward me. I knew this would not go well, and I braced for impact.

I wouldn't have blamed him for tearing into me with some degree of wrath. Instead, he shook my hand and said, "Hi Kent. Do you have a minute to chat?" I nodded sheepishly and we headed back into the now empty sanctuary. I quickly checked out his garb—no tool belt or claw hammer, so I might live through this. As we found a couple of seats and sat down, Rick looked directly at me and quietly said, "Kent, I get the impression you're avoiding me. I've called you a few times, but you haven't called me back."

He paused, giving me the chance to acknowledge his assessment. My mouth was dry. "That's true, Rick," I said. "I'm sorry for that."

He continued, "Kent, you're not only a marketing vendor to me, you're a brother in Christ. Therefore, when it comes to our relationship, I expected better from you, and I'm disappointed."

This wasn't going according to plan at all. At least in the back of my mind, I had figured on the veins standing out in his neck; clinching fists; glaring eyes; ear steam; snarled insults. Then I'd have something to work with. I could redirect the discussion toward his unseemly loss of composure—and in (gasp) church. I could glance at the cross and shake my head sadly.But this was a sly move! He cut off all my escape routes with one deft roadblock. Gentleness! How devious is that? Or—could it be sincerity? I knew Rick pretty well, and of course the answer was clear. This wasn't Rick's first rodeo with an unreliable vendor. I had to figure this was how he handled conflict in business and in life.

All I could say was, "You're right, Rick. I have overcommitted myself and have gotten behind on a lot of things. I apologize that your project is one of them." He responded, "Okay, Kent. I understand. So, here's what I expect. I expect you to find a way to regroup and get back on track. I know you'll figure it out. I look forward to hearing from you soon." He rose, shook my hand, and slowly walked out of the sanctuary.

That was it. He made no irrational demand. He did not insist that I give his project the highest priority. He took no next-step responsibility upon himself; clearly this was my problem to resolve. Most importantly, he assumed the best in me, even amidst this obvious failure. He was calm, cool, and collected—delivering the facts, stating his disappointment, and calling gently for change and resolution.

I stayed in the sanctuary for a few minutes and wrestled with conflicting emotions. On one hand, I was ashamed and highly frustrated with myself. How could I be so unreliable? How could I let a brother down like that? Actually avoiding a man I so highly respected? What an idiot.

On the other hand, I was inspired. I knew even then I had experienced a loving rebuke intended to help me. Something inside me assured me that this is how the body of Christ was supposed to work. This guy was not out to shame, ridicule or belittle me—he simply pointed out my mistake and suggested

I man up. It was a powerful display of maturity and loving correction.

As I reflected on Rick's handling of this situation, two Scripture verses came to mind.

The first: *"Don't rebuke mockers or they will hate you; rebuke the wise and they will love you. Instruct the wise and they will be wiser still; teach the righteous and they will add to their learning" (Proverbs 9:8-9, NIV).*

The second: *"Brothers and sisters, if someone is caught in a sin, you who live by the Spirit should restore that person gently. But watch yourselves, or you also may be tempted." (Galatians 6:1).*

LESSONS LEARNED

I learned a lot that day. First, I learned a key lesson about myself. I have the propensity to agree to too many things, which only leads to stress, frustration, and broken promises.

Overcommitting brings out the worst in me. I had allowed myself to get into that position, and I committed to doing all I could to avoid letting that happen again. More than a decade later, I'm pleased to report no other woodshed incidents like this have occurred (outside the confines of my home, anyway).

Second, I discovered I can handle a loving rebuke. It's a skill I've tried to continue to hone. It's a bitter shame so few people know how to rebuke lovingly, but this experience showed me that if you say it well, I'll take it well. If there's constructive criticism, offered in a way that doesn't get personal, I'll accept it because I want to do things better.

It was good to find that out. And here's the interesting thing. Handling gentle correction has actually helped me handle the not-so-gentle variety. I've been on the receiving end of a few blunt deliveries, and I've redoubled my efforts to take the best of the message and be gracious about the package it came in. I'm not responsible for someone else's tact—just for what I do with the subject at hand.

So much for me. I learned a good bit about Rick, too, and more importantly, the art of the loving rebuke.

First, Rick came to me. I'm ashamed to admit this, but in that first moment in the hallway, I probably would have ducked into some doorway or hid behind the lady with the big hat if he hadn't clearly spotted me. I might have hit the linoleum and army-crawled to the men's room, where I could wait out the danger in a stall.

Pathetic—but likely. This is why it's on the 11th floor of the Hall of Shame, part of the exhibit, "Kent Evans: Wimp or Weasel?" But Rick did see me. And he made the first move.

Second, Rick didn't exhibit anger (on the outside). This is a crucial point. Internally he may have been boiling. He's human after all, and he had left message after message, only to be ignored.

There must have been some emotion there, but he didn't telegraph it. Anger escalates things and causes additional problems. Gently but frankly, Rick got to the only real issue: my lack of accountability. Without a fog of heavy emotions, we could see clearly to face and solve the problem. What a concept.

I've frequently had friends or colleagues seek my input on resolving relational challenges. (Apparently they haven't made it to the 11th floor.) When I dig for insight, not only do I ask whether they've discussed the issue, but I ask how they discussed it. Was it heated? Did my friend become angry? If so, then there really was no productive, healthy discussion.

Third, Rick focused on the core and most important relationship we have—brothers in Christ. That's a factor that should change everything. And if it doesn't, we have some serious questions to ask ourselves.

Rebuke and correction are all about helping someone align to a missed standard. We can't do that unless we agree on what that standard entails. Ours was biblical. Yours may or may not be so, but let's always keep in mind that there has to be an accepted common ground. Maybe it's a contract document or a marriage vow or a house rule. Regardless, we begin with the core agreement and work from there.

Fourth, he had facts (unreturned calls), which led him to a

reasonable conclusion (intentional avoidance). He stated his view and waited for me to respond. He was gracious enough to leave open the possibility that I'd somehow missed his calls. Perhaps he had the wrong number; or maybe my phone had been out of battery for three weeks. Maybe my dog ate it? (Okay, reaching...) Regardless, he left open the scenario, if unlikely, that I was not avoiding him and I was simply unaware of his attempts to reach me. To be sure, he still could have moved on to my broken promise and missed deadline, so there was that. He didn't open our discussion with, "Hey pal, you've been avoiding me!" He began with what was completely inarguable.

Effective rebukers state the facts as they see them and give the rebuked a chance to either admit their fault or explain why the facts have been wrongly interpreted. Most people skip this step and rapidly move through a machine gun volley of facts, interpretation, offense, and remedy. We're dealing from the grounds of relationship, not battle.

Finally, and perhaps most importantly, while Rick certainly wanted the marketing project back on track, he placed a priority on our relationship. I'd go so far as to say that he placed a priority on helping me become a better person. He knew I was wrong, and proving it wasn't going to be difficult. Helping me rebound and recover from my misstep seemed to be his core motive.

This speaks to the heart of the one bringing the correction. The heart of the effective rebuker is to improve the other person. It's a heart of redemption, not ridicule.

When we rebuke in love with the intent to help the other person, we can actually improve and grow our relationships. However, we must handle the interaction correctly, and that's not always easy.

In the end, I regrouped and finished up the project for Rick to the best of my ability—and did so with a certain touch of gladness rather than shame, simply because of how Rick had handled things.

Our relationship became better than it been in the past. I even recall another gracious move on his part. A few years later, Rick took the opportunity to send my wife and me a generous gift card to a local steak house. This guy is the real deal when it comes to leadership and the building of solid, loving relationships. And when there are issues, he turns stumbling blocks into stepping stones. Everyone wins.

I intend to hire him as the roofer for my Hall of Shame—if we ever get to the top floor!

Questions to Consider

• *How have you done as a corrector of others? What's your most vivid memory of that process? Can you look back on the exchange and see where you muddied the waters with your own anger or wrong behavior?*

• *Think back on the last time you took someone to task for their failure. Were you seeking their growth and redemption, or could it be you were just out to vent and condescend? Do you owe someone an apology?*

• *Have you experienced a loving rebuke like the one in this chapter? What did you learn in the process? Have you doubled back with that individual and thanked them for investing in you?*

• *Have you received a rebuke that was true, but delivered in a way that made it hard to receive? Were you able to harvest the good without focusing only on the other person's behavior?*

5

LEARN FROM ACTION

Walk This Way, Please.

There's an old story about a pastor preaching a long sermon in his big, formal, somewhat stiff church. In the midst of it, a raggedy homeless man walks into the back of the room. Then he proceeds down the aisle and sits, cross-legged, on the floor directly in front of the pulpit.

Everyone is murmuring. Which elder will step forward to show this guy the door? I mean, this kind of thing isn't done in a church where the men wear ties and the women wear fine apparel. Why, it's an affront to sacred dignity!

Then an elderly man—an elder, actually, well-dressed and reputable—steps forward, walks down to the man, and bends over. You could hear a pin drop. Then the elder, with great creaking of joints, sits down on the floor next to the raggedy man. And after a moment in which the shock settles in, the preacher continues: "What I've said here, today, few will remember. What you've seen here today, you'll all remember for the rest of your lives."

The best lessons always come in authentic, real-world situations rather than formal teaching. It's just how things work. Take my friend Mark Hancock for example.

I first met Mark at a leadership gathering for the organization he now leads, Trail Life USA. We were in Mt. Juliet, Tennessee, crowded into a room of folks trying to get that group up and running. About one hundred men were there to blaze that trail, so to speak. I sat back to listen to Mark, the CEO, speak to the crowd.

Public speakers come in many flavors. We all love the born communicators who wow you with their delivery: flashy and dramatic and excitable. If they happen to have a solid message, they might just put your brain on spin cycle and change the way you live. Other times, it's so much flash, smoke, and mirrors. You laugh, maybe even cry. Then, a week later, you don't even remember what was said because it was all an inch deep.

Other speakers instantly command your attention just because of their personal conviction. There's something very real in them, and you lean in and perk up your ears. Mark Hancock is this kind of presenter.

Mark was confident, assertive, and bold without being arrogant or demanding. He was magnetic, not because of showy outward behavior, but as a result of an undeniable inward conviction. With a simple and compelling delivery, he shared his heart and his passion for men leading other men, pouring into the next generation. He was unashamedly Christian and unequivocally devoted to the mission of his organization.

Over the course of the next few months, I was privileged to interact with him about a half dozen more times. From brief hallway chats to e-mail exchanges, I had the opportunity to check out Mark in action in a few different settings.

I learned about his background in directing international campaigns and evangelism projects. He was well versed in Scripture, missions, and related topics. Most of all, his character came through. I was always eager to learn a little more about who he was and how he'd gotten there.

Mark had been on the front lines of the cultural divide, sharing his faith with non-believers. He was a godly father, his boys were fun to be around, and his style of leadership was a quietly confident one that I sought to emulate.

I co-founded a ministry that is a proud partner of Trail Life USA, and I connected with Mark and the Trail Life team at leader gatherings in several cities. Every chance I had, I would get myself close up to the Trail Life leaders because I knew that:

(a) These were men of character from whom I could learn much, and
(b) They were leading an organization after which I could model my own.

Mark was compelling enough that it wasn't just about his organization or how I could learn to lead my own. I also wanted to be a husband, a father, a board member, and an all-around guy like him. When you meet someone like that, you find yourself falling into step with him. You look for tidbits you can use in your own experience. In other words, Mark Hancock was a natural and effective leader of people.

As we develop the habit of learning from other men, our learning will come in two forms: direct and indirect. The direct learning is information we hear from them in the form of counsel, wisdom, and input. Indirect learning—generally so much more powerful—happens when we observe their behavior patterns or see them handle particular situations, and we scoop up the lessons intuitively. What people say can change us, if they say it well enough and convincingly enough. What people do will change us, because we see it in the real world rather than simply in the form of rhetoric. Words dance in one ear and out the other. Actions, however, get into our minds and rearrange the furniture.

That's why we need to be proactive in making sure we go where the action is, and the right kind of action. We need to be around the right kinds of life models in their "natural habitats." We see what's genuine and what works. Then we receive deep and powerful lessons in life, sometimes on many fronts at once. Direct teaching tends to be one-dimensional. Indirect, organic teaching can be profound and multi-dimensional.

There's a principle at work in this difference. Have you ever noticed how naturally funny people would rather be funny spontaneously than on command? You grab them, haul them over to a friend, and say, "Go ahead—say something hilarious! Make my buddy laugh!" Then the comedian gives you kind of a funny look, and says, "Um, this isn't a good time." And you think, "Well, gee, what's his problem?"

It's just that some things work better when they arise naturally from life. We can't understand beauty by dissecting a butterfly.

The same thing happens when we want to learn from another man we know. "Go ahead," we could tell him. "Teach me something—blow my mind!" We could whip out a pen and paper and lean forward, only to get a deer-in-the-headlight stare.

This is why our goal should be vigilance in listening as we live, conscious of whom we should look to for life lessons. It's in the application that the learning comes.

Mark Hancock had no idea he was teaching me a powerful concept. He was just doing what came naturally—and for him, what came naturally arose from true-life wisdom.

At one of the conferences, I was approached at our ministry booth by a gentleman who asked me many questions about our ministry's doctrine and theological underpinnings. He was agreeable enough, but it was clear that he was one of those "creed and dogma" guys. There was nothing he would have loved better than for me to raise a point for tasty debate, for which I'm sure he carried an arsenal of Bible verses, theological quotations, and the like. I'm not a fan of verse skirmishes. I know some Christians enjoy the hobby of debating doctrine, but it's not my thing.

We were meeting in a church. During a break, I came across Mark and his teenage son in the hallway. I had my own teenage son with me, so I thought maybe this was a teachable moment for both of us. I'd ask Mark a question and learn something, while my son got a chance to see that lo and behold, his dad actually sought wise counsel sometimes. The moment had potential.

I asked Mark about the theological issue my visitor had raised. I gave him a brief description of the scenario, then said, "Mark, you're well-versed in issues like that one, and I imagine you've encountered all kinds of beliefs in your travels. I don't find it valuable to get into doctrinal debates, but perhaps I simply lack the educational background. How would you handle this kind of thing?"

I knew what followed would be helpful; I just didn't know how poignant and powerful it would be. I was about to learn a lesson on the power of humble deference to someone else present, but I learned it through the specifics of that situation and how Mark responded.

Mark smiled and said, "Well, I have some thoughts on that, of course. But first, I'd love to hear my son's take on your question." And he turned to the teenager next to him.

His son had good genes! He offered a compelling perspective, just as his dad would have done, and even backed it up with a Scriptural reference. He was engaging and confident without being cocky or trying to sound "sophisticated." The answer itself was more than helpful.

Mark, given his theological training and leadership experience, could have done what most people would have in that situation. He could have rattled off a good answer almost without thinking about it. And it would have been a great one.

I would have hung on every word even as it made a positive impression on my son. Good enough.

Instead, Mark perceived an even better opportunity in the situation. He could get his son involved, make it a discipleship training moment, while still helping a friend with an important question. I would never have thought of that. It made me wonder just how many times we're happy with bouncing a solid single through the middle of the infield, when we might have cleared the bases with a home run. Maybe good is the enemy of great at times like that. He knew he could help me, but he swung for the fences and drove home two runs.

When I was in college, I had a roommate who was an accomplished chess player. I enjoyed matching wits, but Eddie was a student of the game. If we played one hundred matches that year, I'm not sure of my winning percentage except that it was right around zero percent, plus or minus. During fall term, he could beat me soundly while studying for his nuclear physics exam, watching a movie, eating a snack, and talking to a girl on the phone. Or at least it seemed that way.

However, as the year wore on, our games took longer to resolve and he had to put more effort into each successive victory. When I saw him turn off the television, put a finger on his temple, and take a deep breath, trying to think more deeply, I knew I was making progress.

My roomie taught me one key lesson about chess: it's not about the move you're making, but the cascade of moves the two of you make after the present move. He taught me to think ahead and play for the next five to ten probable moves. That involves focus and multiple- scenario consideration.

This is what Mark was doing. Rather than make a play for the moment, he was making a play for the future, as embodied by his son. He was also teaching my son, as a matter of fact, and me—a number of lessons.

You may think the story ends there. Mark teed it up for his son who smashed it for a base hit. However, Mark went one step further and taught me a follow-up lesson.

After his son finished, Mark affirmed his son's answer, then offered an additional, non-competing perspective of his own.

"Great point, son," he said after listening thoughtfully. "Kent, what I'd say from my own perspective is that I think that genuine biblical truth is often held in tension between two opposing viewpoints." He held up his hands, visualizing a tight rope pulled between two points, and he went on to explain that the truth was often in divine balance between two perspectives, each of which were simpler and easier for us to grasp.

I found his response equally informative. He succinctly stated a memorable point. He did it with clear, non-pretentious language. He found a space in the subject matter his son hadn't covered, rather than showing up his son by either contradicting it or restating it in a superior way. He just added a salient point that provided his own perspective.

That led to my second major observation: the power of deference. Just because you let someone else share their perspective doesn't mean that you are precluded from sharing yours. You can let others come up to bat and take their cuts. Then, if time and the situation allow, you can step up to the plate as well. In sequencing your comments in this fashion—he goes first, then I go—you even add power and emphasis to your own perspective.

People often listen to you more intently simply because you waited to share, rather than waiting for them to take a breath so you could jump in and hijack the conversation. Deference and generosity enhance influence.

Now let me connect this to my previous comment about direct versus indirect learning. Imagine if I'd walked up to Mark and said, "Hey Mark, can you teach me how to humbly defer to others, disciple my own son, be a gentleman, think several moves ahead, live for the future, show kindness, and wrap all that up with a great and memorable point you would like to make?"

How on earth could he have given me that lesson? Yet that's precisely what he did. It was up to me to ask the right kind of question; it was up to him to be creative and multi-dimensional in his answer. That's the formula for learning in the laboratory of daily life.

If we are to harvest lessons from other men, we must become careful situational observers. In a five-minute interchange with a godly and skilled man, we can gobble up an armload of lessons if we'll only be intentional.

What's even more amazing, this was not something Mark could see coming—no briefing or warning text in advance. I simply bumped into him and lobbed the question at him. And not a softball of a question; I threw him a solid curve by touching on doctrinal debate. His immediate and perhaps even subconscious reaction was to humbly defer and let his son take a shot.

This not only spoke to his methods but his priorities. He was ready to disciple his son at the drop of a hat. Like a trained athlete who hones his skill so well he can execute without thinking, this man reacted swiftly to fully maximize the opportunity before him.

In reflecting on this interaction, I recalled the instructions that Paul gave to the Ephesians, as he discussed how they should walk. He said, "Be very careful, then, how you live—not as unwise but as wise, making the most of every opportunity, because the days are evil" (Ephesians 5:15-16)

The way Mark handled that interaction brought this verse

to life for me. He spotted an opportunity and he took it. A small one? Sure. But, one that now reverberates in my life and my interactions.

Questions to Consider

- *When was the last time you were asked for your opinion on some issue? Did you immediately give it or did you defer to someone nearby?*

- *Do you see your role—as a leader or father or coach—to be to tell others what they need to know or are you there to help them discover what they need to know? What is the practical difference between these two approaches?*

- *Do you make it a habit to observe how great men live their life? Can you think of a time when you observed a valuable lesson from someone even though they were not intentionally trying to provide you with instruction?*

6

FOLLOW THE SPRINTERS

Run, Don't Walk, Toward the Things that Matter

Have you ever felt like you were in the wrong chair? Maybe you were counseling someone through a tough marital situation at a time when your own marriage was reeling. Or you were helping an employee who reported to you set his or her annual goals while yours had failed to launch. Worse, maybe you came to the realization that his annual goals were far more dynamic and ambitious than the ones you were considering.

You were a good soldier. You did your thing, even if you felt the chairs needed to be switched. And you were eager for the meeting to be over, because you now understood that you had some personal work to do.

I had that realization one time in a church committee context. I was blessed to serve for a number of years on our church's ordination committee. This committee operated under the auspices of the elder board, approving or rejecting candidates for the ministry. Ours was a small team of a half dozen men. We took the role seriously. We were not only dealing with someone's heart and passion, but we were judging whether they were ready for the crucial step into a more formalized ministry.

Additionally, we were recommending whether our church should or should not place its stamp of approval on someone. There could be negative consequences for our church's good name if we vouched for someone who flamed out and had a very public failure.

We attempted to treat every man who came before this committee with honor. They were asking to be publicly declared full-time warriors in God's army, a move that subjected them to increased scrutiny and criticism. Their desire to be ordained set them apart and made them worthy of our respect.

I met approximately 30 men in the course of my service, all of whom I admired. They were each in some way my superior; I attempted to fairly and rightly discern their qualifications for ordination. I hope my decisions honored the Lord. All of them were committed, faithful, and godly men. But as I think back these men, one stands out. I recall Dr. Tom McKechnie's interview with a high degree of clarity for several reasons.

First, Tom was older than most candidates. We often saw men who were young adults, but Tom was closer to retirement age.

Second, his was not a typical ministry path. He hadn't received the call in his teens, gone to seminary, then worked in a church setting for a few years. Rather, he'd been an emergency room doctor for several decades, coming to know the Lord later in life.

Third, he was highly poised with a quiet demeanor. We were accustomed to meeting with candidates who were a little anxious, but not so this time. Tom brought a quiet confidence that captured my attention.

He answered our questions capably and succinctly. He described his conversion to the faith and how it was preceded by decades of indifference and even ridicule. He confessed that he'd been less than kind to his spouse (a believer), while being critical of co-workers who adhered to the Christian faith. He carried with him no unhealthy shame, but he was keenly aware of his past and the magnitude of his former failings.

The man had met Jesus. Then, his eyes open to the truth of the Gospel, he dove in without looking back. He'd become an active part-time missionary, logging thousands of flight and road miles to travel around the globe, sharing his faith in conjunction with his medical expertise. In the year leading up to our discussion, he'd been on a dozen international mission trips, leading groups to help establish medical clinics in the name of Christ. This was no typical candidate for ministry; God was already touching people in great numbers through his life and work.

One thing our committee watched for was the degree of accountability candidates had to their families. It's too common for ministers to become engulfed by "kingdom work" while letting their families suffer. Once their families have been damaged, their ministries shortly follow. Therefore, we often asked candidates to describe how they were balancing their ministry work with their responsibilities at home.

But Dr. McKechnie was a bit older. He had adult children, out of the house, so problems weren't in the forecast in that area. Additionally, he had a godly and faithful wife who ran a superb home while he was gone, either during his long ER shifts at the hospital, or as he traveled overseas.

Even so, I felt the need to dig a bit, so at one point in the interview, I asked, "Dr. McKechnie, you have clearly jumped into Christian service with both feet. That's inspiring for me. With all your international travel and your responsibilities at work, do you ever wonder if your family time is suffering?"

Feel free to judge me for that question—the fact I asked it at all, how I worded it. Go ahead, it's a valid consideration. Yet I felt the question needed to be asked, and that was the best way I knew to tee it up.

Dr. McKechnie's response was unforgettable. His choice of words and attitude were impressive. "Kent, that's a fair question," he smiled. "I spent many years running from the Lord and working against Him. I'd like to take whatever remaining time I have on this earth and serve Him with all my heart. I want to find myself sprinting into heaven."

Did you catch those last three words? Did they catch you? They definitely got wedged into the little wheels of my mind, and they've never actually worked themselves free. I found myself turning them over, examining them. Sprinting into heaven.

Three words opened the possibility of a whole different existence—one that had major implications if I were to look in the mirror. The phrase was piercing, convicting. He was not suggesting he'd run himself ragged and leave nothing for his wife and adult children. He was simply saying that whatever he would be doing between now and death, he was committed to doing it with passion, commitment, and at headlong speed. When the time came for him to die, he wanted to be found stretching for the finish line with every muscle—not trudging along or, worse yet, standing still. He'd seen the prize, and nothing was going to stand in the way of his charging after it for all he was worth.

Now I knew why he was calm rather than nervous during that interview. It was a matter of focus and utter conviction. He had boiled life down to its simplest formula: Sprint toward heaven. Follow Jesus. Now. Completely. No looking back. Everything else, including the committee before him, would sort itself out accordingly.

I tried to stay focused on the interview, but my thoughts turned inward for a time. I felt small and sheepish. I was pretty sure I wasn't sprinting. What ground speed would the sacred stop watch have clocked for me? Did I even want to know? Could it even be I was stuck in the starter's stance while the other athletes had taken off, leaving me in their dust. Yet here I was sitting in judgment of a world-class sprinter.

God immediately gave me a picture that helped to cement the conviction I was already feeling. In my mind, I compared Tom to the apostle Paul. And I was some anonymous committee guy asked to evaluate an authentic Road to Damascus apostle, one of God's frontline warriors.

I placed myself back in the first century, when Simon Peter would place a rugged hand on my shoulder and say, "Hey Kent, quick word. We hear there's a new convert making waves over in Antioch. Used to go by one name, switched it to another; dude claims he had some big vision while on a business trip, and, you guessed it, heard from The Man himself. Go and check him out, will ya?"

Then I saw myself strolling up to Paul, with light and holiness just pouring off the guy, and I blurt out, "Paul, my man: I appreciate the way you're creating a stir talking up the Resurrection and all that. I mean, you're taking beatings, launching churches, crossing cultural and language lines—good stuff! But here's a question for you: Would it make more sense to balance this worldwide gospel expansion thing with some chores around the house, and make sure those tents of yours are better quality? I mean, look at the top stitching here. Really, is this your best work?"

I know it sounds absurd, but that was the dialogue of the in-flight movie inside me, as my mind cruised above the altitude of a church committee meeting. Maybe God was the director of the film, and I was catching his message. Sometimes he uses my own wild imagination to help me peek over the horizons of my own arrogance. I call it a spiritual spanking; he calls it mercy.

This interaction with Tom left an indelible impression on my heart and mind. At the time, I was in my late 30s and Tom was my senior by a couple of decades. He felt as if his time was short and the clock was ticking loudly. I realized that my self-perceived status quo was a whole life yet to live, and I could take my sweet time getting to those things which God had called me to do. But what if I'd been jolted into faith the way Tom had been? Would I feel so little urgency then? It wasn't a matter of age, because none of us know when the final tick of that clock will come.

Three words from him had turned my self-concept upside down.

I don't share this story to create a comparison-based metric by which we measure our spiritual progress. The moral of this story is not for you or me to become the Apostle Paul or Tom McKechnie. It's to be the version of you or me that God intends. Simply being a faithful husband and intentional father might be precisely what God has asked him to do. Or sure, the Lord may call you to travel a million miles and set foot on every continent. The product of our faith will differ wildly.

What can be laid on the spiritual ruler for comparison is our level of conviction. Gifts differ, but there should be no difference between Tom's level of conviction and mine or yours. We're all supposed to be in a full-out sprint, based on whatever quality of legs and lungs we possess.

Colossians 3:23 says, *"Whatever you do, work at it with all your heart."* You may not be as fleet of feet as Tom; I know I can't even find my Adidases most of the time.

But both of us have hearts we can turn over to heaven, without reservations or restrictions. Once we do that, we might be surprised just how fast we can run.

LESSONS LEARNED

This interaction with Dr. McKechnie helped me see a number of things.

First, I needed more passion and conviction in my life. If God gave me a task, then I needed to give that task priority within my mind, heart, and on my calendar. My mindset suggested I had plenty of time to get on with God's assignments for me. However, for each and every one of us, that heavenly finish line could be right around the bend. Our mortality stalks us with unrelenting drive. This moment, this place, this task deserves all we can put into it.

Second, I was reminded that questions elicit insights. Even though my question may not have been worded perfectly, it caused Tom to share what was on his heart. I was not trying to be critical or act as if I had caught him walking inappropriately. When we pose questions that display a heart seeking to understand, we tend to get responses that help us learn, grow and change. Reread that one. When we pose questions with a heart to understand, we grow.

Third, there are modern-day Pauls among us—men who have gone some appreciable portion of life rejecting God, only to find their way late in life. Yet, in spite of their godless years—especially because of their godless years, and the intensity of what built up within them over that time—they become faith warriors of fantastic power. It would be wrong to say that believers had given up on Saul of Tarsus; that would be too kind. From the Christian perspective, he was the terrorist of his time. He was a key, violent enemy of the Way. His very conversion was a million-to-one longshot. His becoming the most significant and far-reaching Christian leader post-Jesus was a sheer impossibility.

Look around you. You'll see a Dr. Tom or two, someone unfriendly to the gospel; someone you might have given up on. Know this: God hasn't. He may very well have a plan for amazing redemption, kingdom breakthrough stuff, with that very person at the center—whether you approve or not!

Open your heart and begin to pray for "the least likely of these."

Questions to Consider

• *Have you ever interacted with someone moving at a much faster pace than you? Perhaps it was in work life, in their marriage or in the exercising of their faith. In that light, did you ask them about that speed or trajectory?*

• *Have you ever needed to be on a committee that meant you evaluated the qualifications of people, many of whom were your superior in some way? How did that experience change you?*

• *Is God calling you to take some next steps swiftly and with conviction, but you are not obeying? Why not? Is fear causing you to stand still when you should be moving forward?*

• *Recalling Tom's phrase, "sprinting into heaven," does that describe you right now? Does it describe someone you know? Can you grab a cup of coffee with that person soon and learn from them?*

7

WELCOME KINDLY

Be a Door Opener for the New People

o you have a good memory? Can you actually recall anything you read earlier in this book? Hey, if you zoned out for a few dozen pages—it's cool. Just so you've already paid for the book, man. It's your dollar.

Seriously, you might remember we started with one story in my life that launched all the ones that followed it. That was my trajectory-altering counseling session with Weldon Fuller, in which he told me I couldn't be The Un-something. Instead, he set me on a life course of learning from other men. The next few chapters illustrated a few ways that happened in my life; variations on the theme of watching and learning.

We've made it through six chapters together, so I figure this is a good time for a little change of pace. This next story is something a little different, but it might offer you something usable as well.

I grew up on the south side of Louisville, attending a Catholic elementary school just a few miles from my home. This school carried us through the eighth grade, so most of us fed into a handful of Catholic high schools in the surrounding area. I'm not sure why, exactly, but toward my early teenage years I became convinced that an all-boys school was my best choice. Maybe I was just afraid of being shown up by a girl in class. Who knows?

Whatever the case, I was cut off at the pass. The closest all-boys Catholic high school had just gone co-ed, merging with an all-girls school. We knew of another all-boys Catholic school across town with a great educational reputation. So with the support of my parents, I decided to take the leap and attend St. Xavier High School.

It was a significant choice, and I wish I had time to tell you all the reasons. (You'd probably zone out again.) Suffice it to say, St. X, as we called it, offered me a strong education, good athletics, and high chances of college acceptance. It didn't come cheap, and it wasn't a quick drive, but my parents stood by the choice. Looking back, I realize how they sacrificed to get me the best possible education. I had many experiences and opportunities I'm sure I would have missed otherwise.

All of that to show just a little of my world when I was that age; I wasn't the typical adolescent. Of 400 or so incoming freshman, only a handful of us were from the same elementary school on the south side. Most of the other kids had been friends for a while. They had built their little groups and didn't particularly need outsiders like us. And if you think about being a high school freshman, you might remember that almost nothing is less desirable than being an outsider. Just about the biggest thing in the world is social acceptance, and the biggest fear is rejection.

I came from the proverbial "wrong side of the tracks," in relative terms. We were a solid middle class unit, but my parents had just a bit less disposable income. I was more than a little aware of such things at my age. I even wore a give-me-away hairstyle that screamed, "This kid is not one of us!" Adjustment into my new setting was painful and slow.

I found my place at St. X in two ways. First, I was fortunate to have just enough soccer skill to make the highly competitive team. Sports offered me one way to fit in and develop a core group of friends who looked past the social, geographic, and economic barriers.

Second, I found a friend of friends. This was a kid who didn't get caught up in the superficial values of our age group; he had no love for cliques and social competition. He seemed to be a truly kind-hearted guy by nature, someone who liked everybody and was liked by everybody. How much easier would adolescence be if we had just a few more Andrew Mastersons to go around? He certainly made a difference for me.

Andrew came from an interesting family. His mother and father had gone into the restaurant business, growing Masterson's Restaurant into a very popular dinner and brunch destination in a charming part of town the locals called Old Louisville. Andrew grew up in the kitchens and service hallways of their sprawling foodservice compound, and by the time we met, he was old enough to be frequently pressed into service at the restaurant. Evidently it was great training in dealing with all kinds of people. He and I became close friends.

I recall spending many a late night in that restaurant just goofing off, doing stuff we generally had no business doing. My belated apologies to the entire Masterson family for the broken glasses, the dents in the walls, and the profits drained from all the free Cokes I snagged. Andrew made me do it!

If you know anything about the restaurant business, you know that while the dining room is glamorous, warm, and inviting, the kitchen is just a lot of sweaty, hard work. Having seen the backside of this business, I gained an appreciation for how hard those men and women worked so the rest of us could enjoy our food and soak in the atmosphere. A tip o' me cap to those of you who have worked in the foodservice business.

In that light, Andrew was unique. He was one of the hardest working young men in our whole school. He hadn't been pampered in any way during his younger years. Rather, ever since he could lift a crate of glasses or drag a banquet table down the hall, he'd been put to work. Nor did he begrudge it. He clearly understood how hard his parents and siblings worked, and it was important to him to get busy and do his part.

This combination of old-fashioned work ethic and a family business created a strong, capable, and honest young man. He was magnetic. Virtually everyone in our school loved—still loves—Andrew and his family. I checked him out on Facebook, and he has about a zillion friends. Same old Andrew.

I wasn't going to be one of the cool kids. From day one at school, I understood that was just how it was. Having a friend like Andrew made it so that didn't matter so much. Friendship is a powerful thing, even for lost and wandering adolescents; especially for lost and wandering adolescents. Andrew did me the high honor of welcoming me into his sphere of influence.

As I saw immediately, he was one of the cool kids. Nobody made fun of him; nobody excluded him. Like a prestige credit card, he was accepted everywhere. And anyone who was a friend of his was a little more likely to be accepted, too; almost cool by association, if you can dig that. Sort of an honorary cool kid. And to a brand new freshman from the wrong side of the tracks, that was no small thing.

LESSONS LEARNED

Friendship bestows life lessons. Andrew's friendship certainly did that for me.

First, I learned that young men and women who are put to work tend to develop a strong work ethic. I know, shocking but true. If we coddle our children, they tend to become spoiled brats. Giving them responsibilities, chores, and customers to serve builds character.

Second, I discovered something disturbing: I was as prejudiced and judgmental as some of my classmates. And here I'd thought they held the monopoly on those things. They were judging me as being from an inferior address, but all the while, I was judging them just as harshly for being self-centered and aloof. They saw me as an outsider; I saw them as snobs. And nobody had an open mind for anybody not in their clique.

To be fair, Andrew was not rolling in a daddy-donated Mercedes Benz. But relatively speaking, he and his family had far more resources than the Evans clan. So at first, he was "one of them." I lumped him in with all the gatekeepers of social acceptance. But then things went off my script. He was kind and accepting, breaking through my defenses and teaching me a little lesson about judging books by their covers.

Third, I saw firsthand the power of positive association. Ignore for a minute the unfortunate factor of cliques, and there's still something to learn. The fastest way to get inside the loop is to become friends with someone already there. Or the converse: The fastest way to help someone and make a difference in his life is to sponsor his acceptance into a new sphere.

In this light, I've tried to model this behavior. In many environments, while I may not be the "cool guy," I may have more experience or connections at first. I know what it's like to be on the outside looking in, and I can help others by getting them connected.

It's not just a duty I perform. Rather it's fun and rewarding to help others get their bearings, make friends, or find new opportunities. Just this week I shared coffee with a friend who is job hunting, and he was thanking me for opening a couple of doors with men I know in the industry he is pursuing. In fact, in his case, he mentioned the inbound marketing and web industry as potential fits—relational fastballs right down the middle, given my career path. It's fun to swing for the fences, and it thrills me to help men get connected, especially when they are at a point of need. I consider it a sacred privilege.

Perhaps the most important lesson to take from this story, however, is found in the timing of what I learned and when I learned it. The great bulk of my life lessons came once I had counseled with Weldon, who opened my eyes to the art of listening and learning from others. But this one came when I rolled back the tape and reviewed events from the past, picking up now on what I should have gotten out of it then.

And I'm not the only one who can roll back the tape. That's right—in terms of life education, a whole new course of studies just opened up to you. The past, as Faulkner said, isn't really past. It lives in your memory for your review and reflection. You'll find lessons there that only now become clear and useful. Only later did I understand all the things I learned through my friendship with Andrew.

So roll the tape again! There's no telling what you might find there. As we discussed in the introduction, ours is a nation of isolated men who don't naturally learn how to engage one another and glean wisdom. Sometimes, as life opens us to doing better, we can still learn from all that is behind us.

Consider that teacher from grade school: what did he or she help you realize? Your high school football coach who held those after-practice sessions on character development: What did you overlook the first time around? Your college roommate who had the disciplined study habit: what tips and tricks did you miss in watching him pound the books? Your first boss who showed you the ropes: what positive aspects of his leadership style can you now emulate?

Sure, your life is bigger than a football game—it's a lot of years, a lot of relationships, a lot of issues all crammed together in living memory. But don't be overwhelmed. Take some time to walk through the story you've lived. Think of the people you've known and the places you've been. What you're likely to find is that the lessons and fresh revelations spring up and present themselves to you. "Wow," you'll say to yourself, "I never thought of it that way until now."

Below I have listed a handful of folks from my past who taught me something retrospectively. Maybe this list will jog your own memory:

- My own dad (workhard, fix stuff)
- High school drafting teacher (go beyond the basics, pay attention to detail)
- Baseball coach at age 12 (always try, even if you fail)
- Religion teacher "Crazy Daisy" (acknowledge your idiosyncrasies)
- Neighbor down the street (keep my head down when

swinging a golf club)

Where do these latent lessons lie for you? Can you say "latent lessons lie" five times fast?

This book is all about learning from others, so zone in on those men who particularly have something about them worth learning. Some may not even be alive, and how redemptive is that when they can still teach and still help others beyond their lifespan?

Maybe, like me, you can look back on someone from your younger years and learn how to be a friend who unites people with kindness.

Thanks, Andrew.

Questions to consider

- *Did you have a situation similar to mine when a cool kid accepted you and made your life easier? Why not take a moment to track them down and thank them?*

- *In what settings are you the "insider"? How can you be more intentional in welcoming new folks?*

- *Do you have relational connections today that you can leverage to the benefit of others? Can you be a connector and accelerate the joy or success in someone else's life?*

8

EXERCISE TANGIBLE GRACE

Spend It Lavishly—Plenty More Where That Came From

oy meets girl.

Girl avoids boy.

Boy chases girl.

Girl freaks.

Girl floors it.

Boy trails her all the way to church.

Girl cries, “Sanctuary!”

Boys figures he has girl cornered.

Voice from above says, “Checkmate!”

Heavenly Father had designs on boy and girl to put them together.

Heavenly Father wins yet another one.

Heavenly Father’s record is ten gazillion to nothing.

That's the synopsis of the movie they'll make someday—about how I caught my wife and how God caught me. No actual plans for that movie, as far as I know. But it will definitely play frequently on the in-flight movie in my head.

God is much better at chess than my old roommate. He works with all future moves in mind, and he also knows his opponent perfectly. He understood precisely how to draw me in. The famous queen-to-castle move.

The "queen" was a brown-eyed beauty I met at the University of Kentucky (Go Cats!). This young lady was drop-dead gorgeous on the outside, and of course that drew me in pretty quickly. But it turned out she was even more beautiful on the inside. I would have followed her pretty much anywhere, but it turned out she led me into her church, where I then met God. A terrific minister and teacher there helped me to "taste and see that the LORD is good" (Psalm 34:8). But the meal became ever richer as he also gave me my first taste of God's most delicious earthly fruit: his grace.

His name is Monte Wilkinson. He was the college-age minister at a church in Lexington, Kentucky. My initial exposure to him was through the evening Bible studies he led for the students—and I was shocked by what I discovered about God and the Bible. I'd had no idea what was really in that ancient book, given my measly Bible background.

Monte offered lessons about personal relationships. Wait—that was something that actually had to do with real life! He showed what the Bible said about studying, about sex, about jobs, about nearly everything important to me at the time. I sat there stunned, looking from Monte to the page and back again. This stuff was in the Bible? Shut. Up.

Bible study meeting: Come for the girl, stay for the God. The more I attended, the more I found myself on my own time further investigating the outlandish claims Monte was making, that God was actively involved in every little concern of this world, actively interested in everything about our lives, that he actually cared about me. Crazy talk!

I learned that not only did the Bible have a lot to tell me on topics I cared about, it also told me that God loved me deeply and he wanted my life to have a positive outcome with his blessing all over it. Like Paul, who found himself blind in Damascus, the scales were falling off my eyes. I not only found myself pursuing my future bride, but also my heavenly bridegroom.

I began to sense a conviction about my duality of purpose. I was crazy in love with this dazzling young lady, but I was also being courted by a heavenly Father who loved me beyond measure. I realized these two motivations and guilt began setting in. Could I pursue an earthly love and at the same time plumb the depths of the Father's love? Was this even allowed? When would the hammer fall?

Maybe some evening, right in the middle of Monte's talk, the heavenly voice was going to come booming from above as a heavenly spotlight focused its beam on me: "This student is an imposter! His heart is impure! He comes panting after women rather than living water!" And the people around me would gasp and begin gathering stones.

Monte was a classic college-age minister. In the span of five minutes, he could go from discussing a deep theological truth in the book of Romans, to laughing with frat guys about the most recent knuckle-headed thing they'd done, to crying with a young girl who'd been recently dumped by one of the knuckle-headed frat guys. He was affable, kind, a gifted teacher, and a model of church leader I'd never known existed.

I decided it was best to head off the booming-voice/ floodlight/stoning scenario by assigning Monte as my referee. I asked him if we could have lunch sometime, and he gladly accepted.

We enjoyed light conversation as we sat down and became more acquainted with one another. He knew I did not ask him to lunch just for chit chat, so as we hit a lull in our dialogue, he asked me what was on my mind.

I guess I was testing him, pushing the envelope to see how he would respond. I laid it out there directly: "Well, Monte, I have a question for you. See, I'm really only coming to church because I like April, and I want to be around her."

I paused for a moment to catch his reaction. Which was a poker face. No surprise; I doubt this was his first lunch with a college guy asking about a girl. "So," I added. "Is that okay?"

Monte had a great sense of humor. He looked at me with a grave demeanor and said, "Kent, I won't lie to you. There are higher motives."

We both laughed. "But I'm just glad you're coming at all," he said. "You keep on coming regardless of the reason, okay?"

I agreed and we had a fun lunch together. I don't recall the rest of our discussion, but I have fond memories of the manner in which Monte engaged me and seemed genuinely interested in my wellbeing, the way he could handle my directness without being judgmental.

I wish I could say the skies opened up and I heard a divine voice that day as we downed our burgers. Didn't happen. As a matter of fact, many years passed before it occurred to me how important that interaction was. I believe I was in my 30s, and I was retelling this story to a friend. As I finished, I said, "Yeah, I guess that was the first time I ever experienced grace from any kind of minister or religious authority."

The words leaped out of my mind and onto my tongue. Then I stopped and heard what I just said. Was this true? Had Monte shown me grace? If so, that was a significant moment in my life.

Yes, I decided; he had indeed shown me grace. I challenged him as a symbol of Christian rules and values; I told him exactly what I had in mind, and put him to the test—the result being that, without pausing or flinching or gritting his teeth, he looked past my unworthy motives and said, "Come on into the circle. Come and be accepted."

It wasn't about what I had to offer him; he wanted me to have what they could offer, on whatever terms. For me, that was new math. He took the numbers I threw at him, crunched them, and came to a different total than was expected of "those Christian types."

This meant I didn't have to wear any masks. I didn't have to try to play along with any rules I wasn't ready for. I could come, be myself, and be accepted. Had I gotten the wrong ideas about this kind of place—these people?

Even now, with that encounter 25 years behind me, the memory still brings deep emotions when I revisit it. God wanted to send me a love letter, and he asked Monte to hand-deliver it. Why? Because Monte had read that letter himself once. It was time to pass it to the next guy.

Monte acted out of a genuine love for people and also a firm grasp of the grace he had received. He knew we've all sinned; we've all fallen short of God's glory. (Romans 3:23) He recognized deep down that he and I were more similar than not, both fallen individuals in a messy world with selfish motives and dirty hearts. He was not giving me grace. He was redistributing the grace he'd been given.

I wish I could say I've been a model of this grace to others since that day, because now I can see it's something you pay forward. That's maybe the greatest beauty of the whole idea, as beautiful as grace is, in itself. It comes to you, it's wonderful, and you turn around and offer it to someone else. If we all did it, and did it repeatedly to everyone we knew—what would the world look like?

But a lot of people fail to get that. Too many fail to go back out and say, "Tag, you're it," by spreading the grace to the next needful individual who comes along. I've been one of those non-spreaders too often. I can look back and think of occasions when I had grace to give—and chose the lesser way.

Some of those were people I all but set up to fail through the high expectations I shackled them with. When they fell short, of course, I could have been gracious and merciful. But I wasn't.

There's my beautiful bride of two decades, for another

example. I shudder at the times I put myself and my needs before hers.

Then my sons: How many times have I dealt from temper and impatience, tearing into them for forgetting the house rules, or for not being more loving to each other? I've felt what it is to receive grace. By now I should be an expert at offering it.

I'm not trying to tell you I'm a cold, merciless type. I've had my better moments. I've shown some growth, I believe, and every now and then I feel the evidence of God's perfect and beautiful grace breaking through my bumbling attempts to be a godly man. But still I'm just a guy, and I'll never get it exactly and precisely right. I'll never be the Stephen Curry of divine grace, slam-dunking mercy wherever I go. I may never even make the local starting five of my little world.

We have to realize that just because we've learned a lesson doesn't mean we've mastered it. Even after a breakthrough, when we've been powerfully moved by some new understanding, we find it too easy to take the benefits and move on, without letting the work of transformation begin in us. We have an enemy who works 24/7 to undermine all that God is doing; who would seek to destroy, invert, and remove any good lessons we've learned and use them against us.

But take heart. That enemy is destined to failure, because there's a powerful force at work here. Allow me to walk through this briefly. You've been given grace by your heavenly father. So you give that grace to someone else. When you do, guess what happens? If you didn't already know, you'd never guess it—this part is awesome.

Here it is: He gives you more grace.

There's not a point in your life where God's grace reserves are depleted. The more we blow it, the more clueless we become, the faster his grace is dispatched from the heavenly warehouse—without ever bottoming out. It's like the basket of fish and bread by which Jesus fed the five thousand, with leftovers that made great fish sandwiches later. What God gives is never out of stock. As a matter of fact, the stuff grows the more it's put in use.

There are some things God does when we fail to grow. He may extend the consequences of our foul-ups in an effort to wake us, for example. But when it comes to grace, he never says, "I'm so sorry—I just gave out the last box to some old guy in North Dakota -- said some mean things to his wife, you know. He's forgiven, but you'll have to take a number. We're expecting a new shipment next week."

Monte gave me the lesson. I try to imagine him heading out from our lunch, grabbing a cup of coffee with a co-ed as clueless as I was, someone with problems and nothing but questions when it came to God, and Monte saying, "I wish we'd had lunch yesterday. I brought some grace with me when I got in the car this morning, but I just gave it to this skirt-chasing clod named Evans. You could ask him to let you have it when he's done, if he hasn't used it all up. Oh, and tell him I said not to hit on you. Because if he messes up again—no grace for him! One bowl to a customer."

LESSONS LEARNED

When I had lunch with Monte, he knew he could go on a grace rampage. He could throw it around like a billionaire in Vegas (something that probably needs to happen, actually—the grace part, I mean).

Monte knew the answer to the question, "How much grace does God have?" That answer is: an infinite amount. Easy to remember, because it's the same answer as "How much love does God have?" "How much wisdom does God have?" And pretty much every other question about God. But here's what's even more awe-inspiring. As the years have passed, I've come to the conclusion that it's even better than that. By giving grace, Monte actually increased his capacity for grace-giving.

Anything you do, you get a little better at it—and that's particularly true in God's world. The more grace we give, the more God piles it on.

In the Bible, manna—something a bit like bread—fell from heaven to feed the starving Israelites in the desert. Grace is kind of like that, in my opinion. God gives it to us every day, but just enough for our needs. The stuff has no shelf life; it doesn't keep. If we try to hoard it, it goes stale in our hearts. It's no longer really grace. The whole point of grace is to pass it on. You've been forgiven? Forgive someone. You've been accepted? Accept someone. You weren't judged? Don't judge the next guy.

Our own man-made stuff doesn't usually work this way—money, time, possessions. You give them, they're gone. Sometimes God returns them to us in his own time and manner, but still it's a different system. You can't give away a million dollars and count on another million materializing in the safe.

Grace does that, though. It keeps coming back, keeps replenishing itself. Pretty soon it's all over us, dominates us, and people say, "He's a gracious person. I feel God's reality just by being around him. I want to be like that." It happens not because we received grace, however—everybody receives it from God—but because we kept it moving, placed it right back in circulation.

I thank God for that lunch meeting with Monte. I praise him that he gave me the grace to land at that college-age group with that minister at that season in my life. I thank him for reminding me again and again that the reason why I come is not as important as the reality that I come.

God loves welcoming us into his kingdom by sending some remarkable messenger across our path—a kind of angel incognito, someone who exemplifies the way of Christ in a way that is vastly more powerful than any sermon or lesson or explanation could be. That day in Kentucky, over a plate of burgers with a loving pastor, God gave me tangible grace—a grace I want to give others, maybe even become a philanthropist of the stuff.

Questions to Consider

- *Can you recall a time when you were shown grace? How did it make you feel?*

- *Have you extended this grace to others? How did that make you feel?*

- *Conversely, do you remember a time when you could have shown grace but did not? Do you have time and the relational connection to go back to that person and ask forgiveness?*

- *Is there someone in your life right now who needs grace? Can you give it to them today?*

9

FINISH STRONG

No Shortcuts, Buddy!

Hey! You—the guy who opened this book to the ninth chapter, thinking you could just skip ahead and blow off the first few chapters. What's up with that?

Or maybe you jumped to this page because you were simply thumbing through before reading. Whatever the case, I've got my eye on you. You're a rebel, aren't you? The kind of lone wolf who plays by his own rules, reads magazines back to front, and eats the middle of the Oreo first.

If you're taking a walk on the wild side and reading the chapters out of order for some reason, I want to give you a heads up. Before reading this chapter, page back a ways and be sure to read "Chapter 4: Correct Gently." Otherwise you'll miss the full effect of this chapter when I talk about certain issues of mine.

Plus, you don't want to miss the year I was a finalist as a soul crooner on American Idol, my daring exploits in international espionage, and my encounter with strange humanoid creatures in a spaceship hovering over Roswell, New Mexico. Oh, wait. I edited those parts out due to space limits. Maybe I'll get to them in the next book. Still—who knows what you may be missing when you skip chapters? Word to the wise.

On the other hand, I'm pretty sure you'll find out about me being a recovering yes-aholic; how I have a tendency to juggle too many plates at once, watching them drop all around me, catching only two or three shiny and fun ones. My lips couldn't form the word no. I was far better at taking on projects and responsibilities than I was at carrying through.

So I had a tendency to over-commit. With that in mind, let me tell you another one—this one about the good doctor who cured me (for the most part) of my little issue. His name is Len Moisan.

Dr. Leonard Moisan, Ph. D., is not a medical doctor, but a well-educated friend of mine. With a Ph. D. from the University of Virginia in research methodology, he is one smart cookie. His curriculum vitae includes various academic and nonprofit leadership roles, eventually placing him in Louisville at a reputable private university. After that, he launched out on his own. For the last 15 years he has built a nationally known consultancy helping churches and nonprofits achieve their financial and strategic objectives.

The first time I came across Len, he was presenting to a lunch crowd of businessmen. He was engaging, funny, and obviously skilled at his craft. He had recently launched his firm. He spoke with confidence and shared interesting stories and anecdotes. I decided I could learn something from him, so a few days later, I reached out to him to see if we could grab lunch sometime.

Pause for a moment. Please notice the highly sophisticated networking technique I put into play here. They don't teach you this stuff in Harvard Business School. I picked up the phone. I called him. This is a powerful and often neglected form of learning called "asking someone for advice." Hang on to that one.

When I reached Len, I simply noted he had accomplished something I'd like to do, which was owning his own business. I asked if I could pick his brain on that topic and take some notes. Incidentally, I'd learned he was a former elder at our church and a husband for a few decades. So on a number of levels, I figured I could glean wisdom from this man. I wasn't disappointed.

Our first lunch meeting was a blast. Len has an infectious laugh and a sharp wit and we hit it off. Witty people love me;

I laugh well. Being around me highlights their own wittiness.

Over the course of a few months, we developed a friendship, and I found a possible path toward starting a small marketing consultancy. Through the course of starting up that business, Len and I determined he might be able to leverage my skills for his firm, as well as for his clients. He provided capital campaign consulting services, among other things, and he could add in-house marketing and communications services that I could deliver. So, in one way of viewing it, as I stepped out on my own for the first time, Len and his firm became my client.

Eventually, however, my "yes" addiction made me a liability. Sadly, I Chapter Foured again. I was so enthusiastic I became attached to every proposal that came my way, piling it all on like a starving bunny at the salad bar, and I never stopped to consider whether I was overloaded. It got me into some real predicaments. One of them happened when I dropped the ball on a project and made Len look bad with a customer, hurting his own firm's credibility. It was one thing for me to damage my own prospects, but hurting a client's was unacceptable.

Len was frustrated with the outcome, needless to say, and we had a lovely chit chat about the situation over a spot of tea. And by lovely chit chat, I'm referring to a hollering match [on my side], with veins popping out of [my] neck, [my] eyes bulging, spots of [my] tea dripping down the walls, and mothers hiding with their children under tables [from me].

Len had righteous frustration with my lack of follow-through. I had just plain old frustration. I was angry, and I didn't like to be called on the carpet any more than the next guy. But I also knew that my real anger was rooted in my own self-disappointment. I hated not coming through for him and his customer, but I was determined to deflect responsibility and blame other factors—all the immature stuff we sometimes do rather than own up publicly.

Generally, a nuclear meltdown in business is a solid indicator that you're not going to be doing any more business together. The anger cools down, the tea is cleaned off the walls, and the whole subject just makes both sides want to turn the page and move on. Yet happily, in our case, we actually turned the dispute into the foundation of a strong friendship. We found our footing and—thanks to Len's gracious attitude—rebuilt our relations.

Today we're collaborating on business and ministry projects. I look back on the mess I made of that situation, the misery of our confrontation over it, and still I feel a little queasy over the mental image. But I can also say all things worked for the best. Our friendship and even our business relationship survived, and they're no doubt stronger because we worked through the pain and because I, in particular, was able to face my issues and grow through them.

LESSONS LEARNED

They say you gain wisdom from your mistakes. I've always figured that should make me the new Einstein. I've screwed up in pretty much every area I've blundered into. I learned a whole boatload of lessons from Relationship Version 1.0 with Len.

First, I needed to learn how to let my yes be yes and my no be no, as Jesus tells us to do in the Sermon on the Mount. (Matthew 5:37) That speaks to my word being as good as my bond, and yes equals follow-through, as dependable as the sun coming up tomorrow.

For that to happen, I need to put a strong value on my yes before I release it into the wild. That means regulating my commitments more effectively. I developed a habit, from that point forward, of becoming much more diligent in how and when I committed to accomplish something. If you want to know my secret, or even if you don't, later in this chapter I'll share one basic method that really helped me.

Second, with time and some apologies, even strained relationships can find new footing and be even better than they were before. The virtuous cycle of sin, repentance, and restoration plays out well when both parties are open to it.

How cool is it that something beautiful, in terms of character, can rise up and take wing from the ashes of our worst failures?

Third, having a solid reputation is very important for a business person like me—and maybe a plain old human being like me. "A good name is more desirable than great riches; to be esteemed is better than silver or gold" (Proverbs 22:1). Building that level of repute is a daily battle that yields tremendous influence over time.

Len has a stellar reputation not just in our town but nationally with dozens of college presidents, pastors, and executive directors of various nonprofits. He built his good name—which is more desirable than great riches given that it surely yields them—by following this complex formula.

1. Do what you say you're going to do.
2. Repeat over and over.

That's it. He was as good as his word and people learned that, along with his skill and expertise, he brought steadfast reliability.

Fourth, in your own "lovely chit chats," pick on somebody your own size. That is, never go toe-to-toe verbally with a guy who owns a doctorate, knows Scripture inside and out, and is from the south side of Chicago. Do that and you're going down. That guy munches several guys like you for breakfast, after praying a blessing over them in beautiful biblical syntax.

Fifth, ask and ye shall receive. This is one of the core messages of this book. Don't just sit there. Ask the right question at the right time. It unlocks doors.

The manner in which I met and became friends with Len is a key lesson we all need to continue learning. When we see someone who is skilled in their work, we tend to benefit by being around them, often in ways we could never have predicted. Their perspective, wisdom, and approach rubs off and makes us better. The door to learning is always unlocked. We simply need to turn the handle by asking for help.

If you haven't, in fact, skipped most of the book, you've heard an impressive sample of my stumbles, missteps, pratfalls, and brick wall high-speed collisions—and believe me when I say "sample." You might then be surprised to learn that I'm occasionally asked for advice. (Once these stories get out, that may change.) Anyway, I am asked: "How do I open these learning doors? What do I say to the experienced business guy or the wise spiritual leader to get on their calendar and begin a relationship?"

The central technique that has served me best: directness. I try to find their phone numbers or e-mail addresses and I go right up Main Street with something like, "Hello Len, I recently saw you present at the business luncheon, and I realized that you know a number of things I don't. I wonder if I could buy you a cup of coffee sometime and pick your brain?"

Quite frankly, it's just that simple. Of course you need to be sincere and honest. If you're pandering or angling for their time to get something from them later, they'll sniff that out. I dive into more detail on ideas, techniques, and specific recommendations in Chapter 17. (If you skip there now, I'll find out, and you and I will have a lovely chit-chat about it. How do you like your tea?)

Simply because of my personality type, I have to be vigilant about regulating my commitments. Even after learning my lesson, I'll fall back into that trap through sheer enthusiasm and love for my work, if I'm not proactive. One technique I've used is e-mail highlighting. I know this will sound rudimentary, but if your e-mail inbox is anything like mine, you may benefit from my example.

For a season, in order to help me become more aware of commitments I was making, I'd do the following. Whenever I sent an e-mail that included project-related tasks, I printed it out. Then, with a yellow highlighter, I marked each commitment I made and the corresponding time frame for completion. Something about seeing it in my hand made it more real and tangible. I quickly realized I was a spectacular over-promiser.

I'd often find a half dozen commitments in one e-mail:

- "Yes, I'll get the report to you."
- "I will call you Tuesday."
- "Sure, no problem." (Their request had just become my action item.)
- "I can also send you alternate pricing options."
- "I'm not sure, but I'll find out."

I may find those and a few others in a single, three paragraph e-mail. And, I might have sent five or ten e-mails just like that one in the same day. Do the math. By the end of one day I could have easily made 50 commitments without even realizing it!

How about you? Are you committing yourself far more than you realize?

It didn't take me long to realize I suffered from commitment diarrhea. Yes, sure, no problem, I'm on it, and absolutely were some of my favorite phrases. Yet I rarely counted the cost in time or effort required to make good on them. As simple as this may sound, it was a key turning point for me professionally. I became much more effective at committing to fewer things and following through completely.

I recognize this is a sad tale for the high-tech-inclined,

when one of my key takeaways is how to highlight e-mails; e-mails printed out on paper no less. No one will accuse me of being overly flashy.

However, the crux of this story is not my method for becoming more accountable and reliable. It's that through the character and integrity of Dr. Moisan, I was inspired to do so. We all have room for growth, professionally and personally. You may be highly skilled at the age old art of under-promising and over-delivering. I was not.

This highlights a key principle I hope does not escape your notice: some of the ways in which we need to grow are obvious to us; many are not. We often need to have our faces forcibly pressed against the window pane of self-revelation to unlock our full potential.

When we make a habit of getting around other skilled men, there's no telling what we might learn. You may seek business advice from an executive and learn something about dealing with personal loss. Or you may develop a strong relationship with an accountant and snag a powerful lesson on recovering from infidelity in a marriage.

When we venture into the uncharted waters of relational learning, we open ourselves to a world of possibilities. We dive in seeking one thing, yet gaining another. Our hearts and minds must be open to what God may want to impart from each person we meet.

The wise mentor throws the marbles out on the table and we are the Hungry, Hungry Hippos.

Questions to Consider

- *Think of someone you have seen "up front" recently. What did he or she possess that you might want to have? Can you connect with them and ask a few good questions?*

- *Can you think of a time when you went into a situation and were surprised by what you learned?*

- *What "secondary" lessons have you picked up from talented people? Has the truck driver taught you about music or has the school teacher given you tips on living within a budget?*

10

DITCH THE CYNICISM

Or Don't. Like I Care! Whatever.

One of my favorite bosses hails from la France. I had the pleasure of working for Alexis Grenon for a little more than two years in a marketing strategy role for a global manufacturer. He taught me many things, but foremost of them all:

Rule #1.

Early in our working relationship, Alexis and I met in Boston for a few days of discussions with colleagues. He and I were still figuring one another out, while at the same time charting the course for the project and team he'd recently inherited. We found ourselves in a fairly lengthy discussion with a co-worker who, let's just say, had a few (dozen) axes to grind.

The three-hour discussion with the axe-grinder was

exhausting. She was critical, sarcastic, and relentless in pointing out the many ways our company was blocking its (and her own) progress. She raised valid points, but had few suggestions for improvement. All rant, no remedy.

Mercifully, our meeting eventually concluded. Alexis and I headed to the employee cafeteria for lunch. As we sat down, he said, "Kent, I've made my first decision as the leader of our team. We're going to institute a rule. We will call it Rule #1. Rule #1 is this:

There will be no cynicism about our own company.

But you'd have to hear the way he would announce it: "Rhul numbah wohn!"

Darn. Somehow typing it out doesn't do it justice. Call me sometime, and I'll say it just like he did with the French accent.

We both laughed and enjoyed two more days in Boston. Alexis is a delightful man. He has the typical characteristics of a highly successful executive: driven, passionate and très intelligente. (Okay, I'll stop.) He also has an amazing sense of humor. He could get quite a lot accomplished while still having a load of fun doing it.

While there was a bit of humor in this Rule #1 declaration, its implementation was no joking matter. Often, in our team meetings, he would invoke the rule when one of us headed down the bash-the-company trail. The rule was announced with a smile—a lighthearted way of accomplishing something significant and serious. He deeply believed that cynicism and ridicule drained a company of its effectiveness and energy, and he was determined not to let it take root on our team. I wholeheartedly supported him.

Cynicism is an ugly thing, and in recent years it seems to be infecting our whole culture. Sure, the state of the world has contributed to our spirit of pessimism. We look at anything and everything through the eyes of "Yeah, right. As if." We're disappointed with things, we expect less, and pretty soon most of our words drip irony. But we need to be better than that. A cynical spirit speaks to a lack of conviction that God is still in control, that his grace is still infinite, and that he is working all things for our good.

It's also a simple matter of bad business practice. Negative talk is a virus that spreads through an organization. It drains positive energy from the whole company, and ultimately our customers and clients pick up on it.

So I was all in with Rule #1, putting the kibosh on corporate cynicism. Yet I'll admit there were a few times—particularly via e-mail—where Alexis posed a question that challenged my ability to look on the sunny side of life without being utterly dishonest. The only fitting response I could muster was, "Rule #1 prevents me from commenting." It became a shorthand to express some degree of frustration without dwelling on it or multiplying the problem. But that in itself was positive. We subtly acknowledged real-world problems while underlining the fact that we were committed to a can-do attitude with our team.

My statement said, "We're well aware of the obstacles, but we're going to work through them without letting our attitudes go sour."

This one lesson is a key that can go a long way in unlocking our leadership potential. Guess who enjoys being around complainers? That's right, other complainers. Negative bosses and colleagues attract negative talent who suck the organization dry of its passion for achievement. Cynicism is a self-perpetuating downward spiral toward ineffectiveness.

By contrast, guess what happens to the stubbornly positive? Others begin to follow them.

In this light, Alexis was able to accomplish much while building strong devotion from his team and admiration from his colleagues. Alexis had a stellar reputation for being both winsome and effective. He showed the best leaders were not one or the other—but both.

Alexis was a master at the art of influence. He would verbally dance and gently debate with you until you stopped, looked down, and realized that you were standing right on the spot where he wanted you. And, all the while, you enjoyed the dance.

One of Alexis' favorite phrases began with, "Do you reckon." As an aside, there's a word we don't see too often in our own world. Reckon. It was enlivening to hear it so frequently uttered by this well-heeled Frenchman. Maybe he watched too many old-time westerns on TV: "I don't reckon them cattle rustlers are comin' back, Roy."

But Alexis used "do you reckon" as a subtle way to steer the conversation. He'd say, "Do you reckon this approach could cause us any difficulty in the future?"

Or he might dig a bit deeper with, "Do you reckon that, with this strategy, we could be accused of being out of touch with customers?" If you're struggling to follow his English as a second language, allow me to translate: "Do you realize how crazy your idea really is?"

See, what Alexis realized is that arguing a colleague into submission defeated the overall purpose of leading within a large organization. You literally could not win on your own. You needed allies, and allegiances were not effectively forged with heavy-handed tactics. In the end, if you won the argument but lost their support, you'd lost the most important battle: the battle for the person's willful and active support. This is a lesson most (particularly American) business leaders would do well to learn.

Have you ever been in a work situation where you found yourself at odds with a colleague or a boss? In the end, were you forced to comply, against your will or even better judgment, just because that person had leverage over you? Either she was the big boss, or he had connections with the C-suite, and when all was said and done, you had to toe the line, but you did it with clenched teeth.

This is often our approach and, in my experience, one that is more prevalent in our Western culture. We decide one particular path forward is the only reliable course, and we set out to take the hill, guns blazing. Along the way, we get caught up with intra-company squabbles, while forgetting that the real enemy is outside. We become embittered toward any colleagues we deem as obstacles to victory. Then, when things don't go our way, we complain and gripe about the corporate machine or church politics or administrative roadblocks.

At this point, cynicism and contempt can take root. These are like a cancer within a team, church, or company, and they must be eradicated at the first observance. If allowed to go unchecked, they infect the whole organization, shoving it into a smelly gutter of mistrust and inefficiency.

Alexis was not some wide-eyed optimist, ignorant of our real and tangible internal hurdles. He just refused to dwell on them. Instead, he forced us to imagine—by way of humor and fascinating discussion—how we could get over, around, under, or through them. Nor did we have time for a bellyaching session about the obstacles and why we had to face them. We needed to agree we had a challenge and get right to work on being victorious over it. Not even a moment of cynicism would be allowed.

Along the way, he insisted we engage and activate the positive support of our colleagues in every possible manner. While some colleagues or policies truly did stand in our way, they were few and far between. It's amazing how effective this strategy is: When you look like you know where you're going, and you're excited about getting there, people fall in line behind you. A lot of the original obstacles seem to melt away.

Alexis helped me see that often the barriers to my success are like shadows on a child's bedroom wall. They're not real, but the longer we dwell on them, the more menacing they become, the more power they build. We begin to act in a self-created reality where everyone is against us, and soon we're actively pushing toward our demise.

The truth is, most people are just trying to get their own job done and their goals may not naturally align with our own. We do ourselves and the organization a great service to try and mesh those (sometimes competing) objectives without the destructive addition of cynicism and ridicule.

LESSONS LEARNED

Cynicism divides and deflates. Optimism inspires and engages.

I was often in contact with dozens of other colleagues who knew Alexis. Each one had tremendous respect for his leadership and effectiveness.

This taught me that positive approaches work even within a large company—and it delivers tangible bottom-line results. Particularly in America, we tend to buy into the myth that if we're going to win, somebody else is going to lose. And that's about as cynical a philosophy as I can imagine. It's also incorrect, because it wins battles, but loses wars.

We can create more leverage and more success by engaging people from a positive perspective rather than forcing their compliance through power plays. What we're doing is finding a way for both sides to win. That's a philosophy of hope, the opposite of cynicism.

I also discovered that Alexis' approach unlocked the strongest sense of commitment and creativity on my part. I wanted to do a great job because I wanted Alexis to win. His positive energy caused me to give my best.

While we do sometimes need to mete out consequences

for missing the mark—as parents or leaders—we should do that sparingly. More often than not, we need to rid our homes and our teams of negativity to open up the widest doors of opportunity. Just identifying problems is the easy part. We need to find solutions. That happens only when our brains are fully engaged. This level of engagement comes fastest with an environment of respect and positivity.

Then I learned this incredible truth: French guys can have a great sense of humor. Who knew? Sacre bleu!

Proverbs 15:15 tells us "the cheerful heart has a continual feast." Be positive and dig into the banquet.

Questions to Consider

- *Would your peers describe you primarily as one who points out the problems or offers solutions?*
- *What are your top roadblocks in your job today? How can you work toward overcoming them?*
- *Do you manage a team? If so, what percentage of your time do you spend ridiculing or cynically complaining about the "way things are" around here? What do you think it would do to your team's effectiveness if you cut this time dramatically?*
- *Why do you think it's so easy for us to get wrapped up in complaining about the barriers to our success?*

11 ASK ARTFULLY

Implement a More

Effective Delivery System

Maybe you turn off your cell phone sometimes—at night, in church, at funerals, or—grudgingly—when they nag you about it before an airplane flight. But here's a tip: don't turn your life lesson receptors off. You never know when a nice-sized chunk of Grade A wisdom might come out of nowhere. As a matter of fact, some of the choicest ones come in the most unlikely of places.

You might get your hands on one even, let's say, at the Chili's To Go restaurant in the St. Louis airport. Have you been to that one? They have great cheeseburgers and generous portions of life lessons.

I was traveling with a colleague and we had a bit of time

before our flight, so we snagged a quick bite at that very place while we listened for the boarding call. Except this man was not just any old generic colleague. He was the founder and chairman of the company for which I worked. His name is Jim Headlee.

Jim is a special man. Not only is he a successful entrepreneur, but a devoted husband, an engaged father, and an active member of our community. Along with all his impressive business accomplishments, he has served on various boards and committees helping ministries and missionaries expand their impact. During my time working in his company, I learned a number of lessons from him, most of them indirectly. I just kept my eyes open and watched how Jim handled problems. But, on this day trip, I had some of his undivided attention and our conversations drifted between various topics—faith, work, priorities, and family.

I don't particularly recall how we broached the subject, but at one point we began discussing my family—both the one I was leading and the one that produced me. I shared some stories with him about my upbringing, and I indicated a touch of regret that I hadn't had the opportunity to know Jesus earlier in life than college.

Have you ever been talking with someone and realize that that they are way ahead of you? I'm talking about that chess thing again— some people seem to anticipate your moves, and they're nine or ten moves ahead, but since this is just a friendly conversation and not chess, it's impressive rather than annoying. Jim could listen to what I was saying on the surface level I offered it, but he could see where I was going, too—he could cut through to the true issue, the foundational principle. He listened in layers.

Most people flit around the surface of things, maybe even with their mind elsewhere, and are content to exchange lazy, superficial conversation. I'm impressed by people who understand what our talk really represents: a passageway to the places where our real issues, hopes, fears, and questions are. And they can use that conversation to break through to some of those questions and help us grapple with them.

This was one of those conversations. When it started out, we were two guys at Chili's, waiting for a boarding call. Then, at some point, we were two guys at the intersection of real life and real questions.

As Jim guided the conversation along with deft questions, I responded. Like a skilled captain, he steered our discussion into deeper, more personal waters. From this man, I could have gained wisdom and knowledge across a vast array of topics, among them: running a business, selling, coaching, hiring great people, or personal financial management.

The list could go on. Providentially, we ended up discussing fatherhood, and that's where Jim's intuitive grasp inspired him to deliver the day's lesson. It was powerful and life-changing for me. But you already know that, because here you are reading about it in a book.

I was talking about my father, a man I respect and love. As I hope I've made clear, I'm one of the lucky ones who was born to great parents. But I was also delving into that growing-up period of my life, and expressing my dissatisfaction with one aspect of it. Something, I explained, had been missing. I wished I'd had more spiritual direction from my dad. I'd come to a position of committed faith, but I regretted I hadn't gotten a head start.

Maybe you can relate. You've looked at the picture of your childhood, and you've seen it was a jigsaw puzzle with just a couple of pieces missing. And you think, "Mom and Dad were the ones putting the puzzle together, right out of the box. What did they do with those pieces? Why isn't my picture perfect and complete?" Then you become judgmental of their puzzle-building skill and harbor a resentment.

I may not have stated it exactly that way at Chili's, but it's what Jim was hearing. And as I moved down that road, he put up an unexpected detour with this question: "Kent, do you know what every father wants from his adult children?"

Wait a minute. This was my story! How'd we get to talking about fathers? Still, I paused for a moment. It was actually a pretty interesting question. I had to admit I'd never thought about it before; I was too involved with the road of thinking about me.

"Hmmm," I said. "I can't say that I do."

Jim said, "Your children are young right now, so you don't yet have the advantage I have. I have older children, some of whom are already leaving the nest. And I think what I want from them is similar to what every father wants. I want my children to know that I did my best. I may not have been the perfect father, so I don't need a lot of praise from them. I don't deserve it. On the other hand, I know I did my absolute best, based on the tools, skills, knowledge, and experience I'd acquired. I used what I had and gave it my best shot. My kids may or may not acknowledge that I was the best father they could've had—but I'd love for them to acknowledge that I was the best father I knew how to be."

Again: Hmmm.

Jim took it a step further, to make the point inescapable. "Kent," he said, "have you ever told your father that you appreciate the things he did right? I bet you could come up with a list of those things and maybe even write them down and send him a letter sometime. Now imagine, as a father yourself, how you'd feel to receive a letter like that from your kids." You know it! I can't imagine a better feeling."

"It would be the best gift anyone can give, the gift of appreciation."

Jim was actually giving me a pretty good gift right at that moment. One thing I loved about him was his teaching method. He could give instruction and advice wrapped in a simple question, which was wrapped in a friendly chat, which was wrapped in a smile.

He was at the same time insistent, yet accommodating. It's easy for teaching to be pedantic, for the teacher to assume a certain high and condescending position. The best of them, however, know how to pull you up rather than put you down, by making a true and warm connection. That's Jim's style.

His comment rattled around in my head for several days. Eventually, I realized I could only make the rattling stop by doing something about it. So I took Jim up on his suggestion. I sat down to write my father a note of thanks for all he did for me as I grew up.

What struck me was how easy it all was. Once I got started, I really enjoyed writing that letter. And the list of the things he did well—the letter wrote itself.

First, I could praise him for the countless hours he spent as my baseball coach. He had a great sense of humor, and often in practice he'd use his quick wit to make a point and offer correction without showing us up around our teammates—a big deal at that age. I can still hear him yell out, "Way to slow it down!" whenever an infielder let one slip through his legs. He was an engaged, energetic, and fun coach. The game is supposed to be fun, and there are certain parents out there who don't always get that.

Second, I could let him know how much I appreciated his work ethic. My dad spent many an evening or a weekend under the hood of one of our cars, prepping the fields at the baseball park, volunteering with a local civic organization, or fixing something around our home. He was not a lazy man. He routinely put his skills to use for the betterment of others.

I wrote these things down, and each one suggested several other things: teaching me how to work with power tools; picking me up from four straight years of soccer practice; sacrificing so I could attend a private high school; and, making me aware of the role of a board member in a nonprofit. Through this process I discovered many ways in which my dad had been a huge blessing in my life, and I compiled them into a letter.

I mailed it, but even as I slipped it into the envelope I was aware that I needed to receive the blessing of it just as much as Dad did. The exercise had brought out in me a new appreciation of my father. I'd had all the pieces, but had never fully assembled the picture. Being able to feel gratitude was good for my heart.

A short time after I'd sent the letter, he came by my house to drop off some tools I'd asked to borrow. He gave me a quick, "Hey, I got the letter you sent. Thanks a lot, I appreciate it."

That was it. Seriously. There was no outpouring of emotion, no commitment to get together for coffee every Friday morning and share our deepest struggles. But I knew what lay beneath the manly restraint. The two of us softened a bit that day. We made one more step in our relationship as we walked through the door of a heartfelt appreciation for the good things.

LESSONS LEARNED

Thanks, Jim.

Not only did he help me improve my relationship with my father, but he gave me one more tool to put in my personal influence toolkit: the art of personal reflection.

Jim's approach was a stroke of psychological and interpersonal genius. What if Jim had said, "Kent, you have officially become a whiner and are focused on all that was wrong in your life. You're an adult now and look at you, still wanting something from your daddy. Why don't you grow up a bit and show some appreciation, you big baby?"

Do you think I would have received that well? No sir. I would have focused on the messenger and completely missed the message. I could have become angry and resentful that he would talk to me like that. I would have learned nothing. And to be honest, I would probably have smarted off and gotten fired again.

However, Jim decided to wrap some advice in a personal story. It would have been blunt simply to say, "Do you know what your dad probably needs from you?" Instead, like a good illusionist, he used a bit of misdirection. He internalized the question and told a story about what he wanted from his own kids. He didn't preach at me, but simply shared his perspective. Then—and this was ultimately the crucial step—he gently suggested I take some action based on the perspective.

For us men, this is a supremely important skill to master. Know why? Because we regularly become frustrated with others for not listening to us. However, upon deeper inspection, we might find that the problem is not their ears, but our mouths.

I am slowly arriving at a conclusion in life. Now, this is not scientific, but I suggest that approximately 87 percent of our frustration that "nobody listens" is directly related to how we share our opinions, advice, or insights.

Put another way, it's highly likely that the reason you're not being heard is because you're saying it wrong! Sometimes a spoonful of sugar does make the medicine go down; a bitter pill, on the other hand, is a little hard to swallow. Presentation counts.

You doubt me? No worries. I propose a small wager.

Take the largest bill you have in your wallet right now. Fold it into your hand. Make sure it's hidden so that it's hard to see what you're holding. Now, walk up to someone who knows you well and trusts you. It could be your spouse, a child, or a coworker. Shove your hand forcefully toward them and say, "Here, I want you to have this." Carefully observe their reaction.

The wager: if they don't recoil, e-mail me the amount of the bill and I'll send you one. If they do as I predict, you send the bill to me.

Do you feel lucky, punk?

You don't even have to try the experiment. Intuitively, you know it's true. However, the trying is fun and teaches a great lesson (especially for your children who are always wondering why their brother/sister "never listens to them"). Even things of high value are rejected when delivered too aggressively.

This is true for those who already trust you. This works even more powerfully at a mall where people avoid you when you get within 10 feet of them. The lower the level of trust, the less likely they are to receive what you freely give. Yet, even high trust cannot always overcome bad delivery.

One point of caution: if you try this at a shopping center, first scan for the mall cop. Skipping this step can cause you to spend a couple hours in a "secret room" with some grumpy people. And, your repeated pleas, "I was only doing an experiment! I really just wanted to give them money—I read this in a book," will fall on deaf ears. And if you give them my name, I will deny everything. I'll say that the book's editor, Rob Suggs, came up with this idea. So don't even think about it.

Not only did I learn to be more appreciative of those who helped me get to where I am from Jim, I learned how to help others arrive at a beneficial conclusion all by themselves. He helped me increase my capacity for compassion and influence.

Questions to Consider

• *Have you ever lamented that the people in your lift (e.g., your kids) just "don't ever listen"? Could this be partly (or wholly) due to your method of delivery?*

• *Can you become more winsome in how you offer up insights and input?*

• *What would happen if you went to your spouse or children and said, "Sometimes I don't think you listen to me, but that could be because I make it hard to be heard. What could I do that might make it easier for you to receive my input?"*

•*Do you have some axes to grind with your parents? Is it possible that you're focused on their failings and haven't given proper consideration to the positive role they played in your life? Do you owe one or both of them a letter of appreciation?*

• *Could this same principle be applied in some other area of your life? Do you need to write a note like this to your pastor, a former or current boss, a sibling, or your best friend?*

Write a letter of thankfulness to your love ones.

12

KNOW WHEN TO LET GO

Get a Grip. Then Turn It Loose!

I signed the guest book at the nursing home—noisily. I was coughing and clearing my throat over and over (Ohio Valley = allergies).

Nearby, Butch Dabney waited patiently in his wheelchair. He had lost many of his physical abilities but none of his razor-sharp wit. He mumbled something, and the only word I could make out sounded an awful lot like—well, casket. Not exactly a happy word for this particular setting.

I looked up as I heard it and said, "Butch, can you say that again?"

He repeated, "That you, casket?"

I was at a loss. With a furrowed brow, I apologized, "Sorry, Butch, I don't follow you."

The guy rolled his eyes at me. Yes, he rolled his eyes,

something not generally part of the 91-year-old's arsenal. He sighed, "I don't normally have to explain this. Is that you, casket—get it?" Then he watched me expectantly.

We were clearly on different pages, and I just stared, clueless. Until he raised his voice and said, with heavy emphasis, "Is that you coffin?"

I almost fell over the reception table busting a gut laughing; one more thing that kind of stood out in a tranquil senior environment. Heads turned. Checkers games paused. Knitting needles froze in mid-air.

Butch was shaking his head in disdain. This Evans kid, 50 years his junior, was too slow for the Butch Comedy Act. Kids today.

Butch wasn't disdainful as a rule. Actually, he was a humble and unassuming gentleman. He did have a rapid-fire delivery when it came to one-liners, so a lot of people dropped 'em when he pitched 'em—even now, within sight of the century mark in age. His eyes still bore the gleam of a lucid and active mind, still curious, still fascinated by the world around him. Just the way I'd like to be if I'm still answering the roll call past 90.

Butch was such a delight to be around that the "Butch list" was often the first to be claimed. What's the "Butch list," you ask? See, we have a team responsible for delivering communion to those no longer able to attend church. The lists were normally ready at midday on Saturday. If you waited too long, the list with Butch's name would be gone. And that was the hot ticket. If you drew communion delivery, why not get the guaranteed entertainment of an encounter with Butch? He was a hoot, but there was something more: he was a man of God.

Our church was founded in the early '60s, and Butch was a founding elder. We recently celebrated 50 years of worship. Butch helped to hire our longest-serving pastor, Bob Russell. Over the years, everyone knew that these two men were more than simply pastor and elder. They shared a deep friendship that can only result from co-laboring in God's kingdom over a long period of time. I imagine nearly every church has "that guy" who is as essential as the columns that support the steeple. Butch uplifted us in much the same way.

As his spirit remained willing, his flesh was weaker, of course. The years caught up with him, and he knew his days of setting the pace were coming to a close. He used to joke, "Of our four founding elders, three have already died and I'm not feeling so good myself." But who could believe it? How could anyone "not feeling so good" give everyone else so much joy? Who else shared so much wisdom?

I was the lucky guy who got the "Butch list" that day, so I

took full advantage by spending time with the great man and his wife. We chatted about subjects of all kinds. At the time, I was serving on a committee with one of Butch's grandsons, and he took the opportunity to get in a little jab, saying, "You guys have Andy helping with communion? Good. Just don't let him help with the finances!" No one, not even blood kin, was spared from his merciless onslaught of one-liners. I laughed early and often, and once again thought, "Lord, let this be a preview for my life. If I can be anything like Butch, then I might not have any problem with growing old."

One of the best parts, as always, was hearing the stories of our church when it—like Butch himself—was younger. "I used to be in the middle of everything that happened," he said. "Now I'm not in the middle of anything."

What facial expression did you picture as you read those words? Probably you imagined those words delivered sadly, with a sigh. Nope. This was not a complaint. This was not the old, "They don't care about me anymore" routine. No, he was smiling, even offering a hint of joy and satisfaction.

Once the church needed him for any little thing. Now it was like a grown child, out on his own, and he could look with the pride of the parent who did the raising. He was grateful. He was fulfilled. And now it was perfectly natural for him to sit back in his wheelchair and enjoy being on the receiving end of the church's ministry.

I learned two powerful lessons that day from Butch.

LESSONS LEARNED

First, as Solomon points out in Ecclesiastes, there's a season for everything. Life is divided into them the same way the week is into days.

To live out our years is to progress through various seasons, each one unique in its way. We have childhood and then youth; we are newlyweds for a time. Then children of our own come along, maybe grandchildren or even great-grandchildren. There's a time when we must visit the sick in hospitals, and later a time when we are the ones being visited. Two sides of a coin, each one with its own place in the great scheme of things.

As these seasons pass, we can either embrace the new one or—like many people—wallow in self-pity, yearning for that season when the "weather" was so much nicer. We all know those who ache for the past and are soured by their refusal to let it go. Then we meet guys like Butch, who show exactly what it looks like to be a man for all seasons.

Second, he showed me that gratitude is a lifelong pursuit, and you have to get that going early. We don't magically turn 80, then decide to hop aboard the gratitude train. If we're grateful in our 40s, we're more likely to be grateful in our 60s and 90s. This is a mindset we don't install, but cultivate. We plant seeds, not a fully grown tree to stick into the ground. Butch's gratitude was the gracious outgrowth of a life lived with the right perspective. He fully understood the blessings heaven had afforded him, and that understanding brightened everything about who he was.

To be clear: I'm not suggesting we put older folks out to pasture once they can no longer drive the church bus or play in the softball league. Butch continued to serve our church well into what many would call the retirement years. His wisdom and candor were routinely sought out by our elders and by Pastor Russell. His tales of God moving mightily in our church were legendary and his perspective never lost its value. Nobody escorted Butch off the field to a padded seat on the sidelines as he aged.

However, I think each of us must realize that at some point it becomes necessary (even advantageous) for us to be gracious and proactive in offering others the mantle of responsibility. Butch seemed content to let us whippersnappers shuttle communion all over the city. He'd spent his fair share of time ministering to our congregation, staff, elders, and deacons, and it was perfectly fine by him to see a new generation step into these roles.

Lessons are like any other kind of treasure. Some of them work like cash-in-hand; we can spend them straight away. Other precious insights, however, must be stored up for later retrieval. They're invested and they accrue interest, more like savings. We get the most value out of them at a future date.

The time spent with Butch provided me with a valuable deposit into my life's wisdom account. Now, in my 40s, I find myself in the middle of many things, too. To name a few: I lead a family of six (soon to be seven); work a full-time job; chair the board of a growing nonprofit; write; teach; coach soccer; and serve as a deacon at my church. I have a number of irons in the fire. But there's fast approaching a day when many of these tasks will need to pass into the hands of abler and more energetic men and women. I pray I am well prepared to make a smooth transition at the right time.

I suspect you can see this today in your circles of influence. You are serving on some committee or within a department at work and the leader is well past his or her prime. He's unwilling to give up control, yet it's painfully obvious that he should at least share the command—if not relinquish it completely ("Bah, that social media thing is a fad!"). There are two reasons he won't yield: fear and pride.

The fear he feels is rooted in his own future. If he lets go of this role, what will he do next? Where will he find value?

How will he have an impact? How will his skills be used again? Will they be used at all? He finds some portion of his self-worth in his service on the team, and if he gives that up, it will be as if he has lost a limb. He views a transition as an amputation of relevance and he will not raise the knife on his own.

The pride issue is similar, but has a unique nuance. Pride steps in and scares the leader, whispering this threat: "If you step aside, things might actually improve. Then what's the message sent? Bingo. You were holding this organization back! You got out of the way and let the good times roll."

Sure, that's a scary proposition, especially if it turns out to be true. Quite often when leadership "freshens up," things do improve. Change tends to help organizations reboot and find new energy; it's just the way of things. Membership grows, profits soar, or the team notches more wins under the new leader. But what made it all possible? The foundation laid by the old guy.

I led a volunteer committee that planned a large annual event for our church. It was fun, challenging, and demanding. I was in my sweet spot. The role was a good match for my skill set, available time, and personal interests. However, in my third year, I saw others on the team who could lead this effort just as capably as I did, and (I suspected) maybe even better.

Right after the event one year, I went to our church staff

leader for the project and resigned. I concurrently suggested my successor, a man already serving faithfully on the team. He accepted the role, and the following year the event was even better and more effective than the ones when I was leader. I didn't see this as a failure, and I'll explain why.

Our church was blessed with one senior pastor for 40 years. An amazing feat for one man to grow into successively complex leadership roles, all the while maintaining his personal integrity and his ability to smash home runs every weekend from the pulpit. As he walked us through his transition from leadership, he shared many powerful leadership lessons—one in particular stood out for me.

During one weekend service, he said the following (I paraphrase): "Some may wonder whether I secretly hope the church loses momentum after I leave, as if this somehow validates my leadership role. I suggest the direct opposite. The greatest testament to my leadership would be explosive future growth. It will indicate that I served faithfully, helped lay a good foundation, and most of all, appointed capable men to succeed me. Nothing would make me happier than for this church to have a greater impact in the future than it has in the past."

It was no coincidence that Bob Russell, our pastor, had spent four decades serving alongside Butch Dabney. For years they'd been friends—iron sharpening iron.

Questions to Consider

- *Are you serving in a capacity where you may be past your prime? Are there capable young leaders chomping at the bit? What stands in the way of you stepping aside and allowing them to lead?*

- *Are you on the other end of the spectrum—you're considering helping out with a key task, but you see capable leadership in place so you are hesitant. Could you engage now and learn from those who have gone before you? Maybe you are the succession plan they've been praying for.*

- *Do you have a close friend who has been holding on too long? Can you lovingly pull him aside and suggest he become more intentional regarding a transition?*

- *Are you secretly bitter and resentful about the work you used to do? Are you harboring ill will toward your successor because he has clearly achieved more than you did? Could you swallow your pride and send him or her a note of congratulations?*

13

PRAY SPONTANEOUSLY

Operators Are Standing By

The London Hilton. May 22, 2014. I peered across a bowl of split pea soup, in the hotel restaurant—dumbfounded, convicted and impressed all at once.

In my life, I have not known many famous people, but I've had a handful of opportunities to meet with influential and deeply experienced people in their field. When I get this chance, I enter a state of hyper-observance and put my antennae sky high to pick up even the slightest hint of a lesson or tidbit that could help me.

I found myself in the heart of London meeting just such a man, a hero of the faith: Rob Parsons.

Don't feel too badly if the name rings no bells with you. For most Americans, it may not. An analogy will be helpful here. Maybe you've heard of James Dobson, the founder of

Focus on the Family. If you were to drop James Dobson in Europe, you'd have Mr. Parsons. At the time of this writing, he's been in full time family ministry for 25 years as the Chairman of Care for the Family, based in Cardiff, Wales.

I met Mr. Parsons in a manner only God could orchestrate. Follow me on this, as there's a beautiful lesson to be learned. Will, a friend from my home town, took a job at Focus on the Family in Colorado. While there, he met Tim, a colleague from New Zealand. Will introduced me to Tim, so Tim and I set up a Skype to get better acquainted. As I talked with Tim, I relayed how God was moving in the Manhood Journey ministry some friends and I had launched. Tim said, "You know, mate (yes, really, I love it!), you need to meet a gent in the UK, Rob Parsons."

Tim didn't know this at the time, but I'd just scheduled a work trip to London, about one month out. So, I leaned in and asked Tim if he could set something up. Tim gladly obliged, and the next thing I knew I was on Mr. Parsons' calendar for lunch at the London Hilton.

I share the connection details of this meeting to underscore a few key points. First, I couldn't have orchestrated all this. Only God could weave such a wild and far-flung tapestry of relationships.

Second, I don't spend much time in London, so the

odds of Mr. Parsons being there (two hours from his home) the same day I was are even more remote. This was no "chance" meeting, and that heightened my awareness of what God might do through it.

I fully understand that God is no respecter of persons and that Mr. Parsons, as it relates to our standing before the Lord, is not some demigod to whom I needed to crawl for just a shilling sir, if you please.

However, if you are going to get financial advice and you can get time with Warren Buffet, it sure beats asking your impoverished uncle. Let's give honor where it's due. Mr. Parsons was more than 20 years my senior and the leader of a large and effective ministry that had been in operation since I was a teenager. As the cofounder of a recently launched nonprofit, I had much to learn from this man.

As our comfortable conversation unfolded, I was struck by how kind yet deliberate this man was. He was friendly and warm. He inquired about my family and the ministry project in which I was involved. I shared the general overview of our ministry, providing enough detail to prime the pump so he could give me advice and counsel.

After maybe 20 minutes of getting to know one another, I figured he probably had sufficient context to speak into our situation. I paused and said, "Okay, Rob, so what do you think? What advice do you have for me?"

What happened next was—well, uncomfortable. Silence. A thin smile. More silence. A sipping of the split pea soup. A bit more silence, topped off with a slightly upward glance that said, I'm thinking.

I'm an extrovert. I like robust, quick dialogue and maybe even a raucous exchange. In fact, to kill some time before my meeting with Rob, I'd rented a self-service street-side bicycle and pedaled across several miles of the historic town. I learned along the way (from a "helpful" Bobby) that I was not allowed to ride on the sidewalk; so I'd trekked around Hyde Park and past Westminster Abbey in the middle of the streets of London. I had no helmet, no stick-on reflectors, and truly had no clue which side of the road the cars should be on most of the time (Whoa! That's no turning lane!). I'm normally high-strung, but at this point, I was Xtreme Kent, fully charged and running at breakneck speed mentally.

Therefore, even though the silence may only have been 10 seconds long, it felt like an hour. I thought I heard a clock ticking across the restaurant and the clink of a cube of ice in my drink as it melted and fell. It was difficult to wait out the response. The response eventually came—only it was no response at all. It was a prayer.

Breaking the silence, Rob said, out loud, "Father, my

brother Kent here wants some advice. But, I know that he doesn't need my advice, he needs Yours. Please give me the wisdom to share with him precisely what he needs to hear."

I was floored. Here was a guy who had been in ministry 25 years. He had counseled with major world influencers. He had a rock solid marriage. His ministry budget was several million dollars and encompassed a staff of nearly 100 people. He had been there and done that. He had forgotten more about ministry than I had ever learned. He carried around in his head lessons, experiences, trials, examples and stories. He had every right to begin his response with, "Well, Kent, in my experience, here's what I have seen."

However, he chose to check it all through with God. He knew our time was short, and even at another point in our discussion reinforced this notion by suggesting that in all likelihood, this would be our only meeting this side of heaven. Knowing this, he wanted to make the most of our time together, and deep down he knew that on his own, he was insufficient for the task. He needed divine intervention to make the next 90 minutes as beneficial as possible, for me.

I believe I could write an entire book just unpacking the wisdom in this single lunch meeting. The list below would furnish individual chapters simply suggested by how this man handled our encounter:

- He was not self-focused.
- He was humble.
- He sought out my best.
- He was painfully honest, not sugar-coating the road that lay ahead for me.
- He gave me practical details regarding the funding of his ministry.
- He encouraged me to write this book (well, a book at least—I won't hold him responsible for this content!).
- He offered his ongoing help and gave me private access to his personal e-mail address.
- He treated it all with deep importance, as probably our only personal meeting.
- He asked great questions.
- He paid me several genuine compliments.
- He was transparent.
- The list goes on.

In short, I was witnessing a powerful clinic on how people should behave at all times, but rarely do. A lifetime of wisdom over a bowl of soup.

But what you're reading is only one chapter, so I have to pick a lane and stay in it. I choose Rob's decision to pray. His prayer was immediate, spontaneous, and unfettered. He didn't need to think about what to pray or the order to put things in. He didn't even need to close his eyes. He just began talking to God, as he'd do for anyone who happened to be sitting at the table—which, of course, was his stance toward God.

I don't want to suggest he was at all insensitive, but I can say this. The most important thing to him wasn't that I was sitting right in front of him. He definitely cared about me—enough that he could look past me and "see" the presence of God, and thus the importance of connecting me to Him. This was a one-time-meeting in which every moment was precious, and for him, the most valuable use of it was prayer. After all, time has limits but not eternity. Rob could help me for a lunch, but God could help me for a lifetime.

This was a gentleman whose organization was called Care for the Family. And he embodied those words.

On a fairly regular basis, some leader falls short of his reputation in a very public way. It could be the politician with the secret mistress, the pastor with the fudged expense account, or the pro athlete struggling with addiction. It's not strange that we've become highly suspicious of anyone in leadership. We have swung the pendulum from idolizing leaders all the way over to assuming every last one of them is up to some hijinks. Just you wait, the truth will come out one day. He can't possibly be all he is cracked up to be.

In his excellent book 7 Men, Eric Metaxas points out,

So you could say that we've gone all the way from foolishly accepting all authority to foolishly rejecting all authority. We've gone from the extreme of being naïve to the other extreme of being cynical.

I realize that if I were to spend time with Rob's wife, his personal assistant, or a long-time friend, I'd discover some clue that this guy puts on his socks one foot at a time like the rest of us. I'm sure that he has become angry, been passive, took a shortcut, or allowed cynicism to creep in. He's a human being, and that means he has sinned and fallen short just like everyone else. So it's not for me to make an idol of him or of anyone else.

However, in our few moments together, I observed an alignment between Rob's ministry goals, his public persona, and his actual behavior—a consistent man in body, mind, and soul. I don't believe he wears one face in public and another in private. What I saw is what I got, and what a goal that is: simply to be who you are, wherever you are, whenever it is, without mask or games or pretense. How powerful is a consistent life?

It's a model for me to emulate.

LESSONS LEARNED

Among the many lessons I gleaned from this experience, I will highlight three.

First, as I've just said, I'd love to be my own consistent self. It's so tempting to play to the crowd—at least I know it is for me. We give the people what they want, and maybe they'll love us a little more. That means I have this "me" for church, this "me" for the workplace, and still another "me" for hanging out with my buddies.

Whether at home with my family, alone in a hotel room, or leading a seminar, I'd like to be as aligned and square as Mr. Parsons.

Second, I'd love to think I'm as focused on whoever is before me as Rob was for me—that when I'm the guy someone approaches for advice, I can be as wholly and genuinely absorbed by their needs as he was with mine. The Bible urges us, "Honor one another above yourselves" (Romans 12:10). Do you always feel honored by people who meet with you? Me neither. That's why Rob—a guy the rest of us would honor—was so striking in how he approached things.

Third, and perhaps most impactful, I'd love to find myself checking in with God as a first reflex. I mean, we should only do something first when it's the best option, right? Checking in with God is always the best option if we're discussing serious matters of everyday life. My default is to blurt out my take on everything. Maybe my take would be a bit more valuable if I'd been checking in first with God all this time. Rob showed me how that works.

I have my own share of experiences, stories, mistakes, and successes from which I can pull to help others. Then there's Rob, whose mountain of wisdom and experiences makes mine look like an anthill. Then there's God, whose infinitely, unimaginatively vast wisdom blows away yours, mine, and Rob's like the morning mist. The three of us—you, Rob, and I—have access to that divine wisdom. It's a prayer away at any moment. How vain am I to hook up someone with my wisdom before looking up to God's? This is a lesson I'm trying to revisit every day.

Questions to Consider

- *When people come to you for help, do you have their best interests at heart or are you just concerned with demonstrating your genius?*

- *Do you see God as one who sets divine appointments, as he did for me in this case? Do you pray for the blessing of his guiding your relationships and opportunities?*

- *Who do you know who could help someone else? Are you the initial contact who could facilitate a beneficial connection?*

14

TAP SHOULDERS

Become a Top Talent Scout

Hall of Fame football coach Don Shula said, "I think what coaching is all about is taking players, analyzing their ability, and putting them in a position where they can excel within the framework of the team winning." Every great coach knows that discovering potential and aiming it correctly is a key to winning. Every pastor knows it, too. We "lay" people must also grab hold of this and do our part. We need to tap a few shoulders.

I met Kurt Sauder when he came to our church as our first men's pastor about 15 years ago. He blazed a trail at our church as he shepherded and guided our men in a powerful and passionate manner. He was (and still is) an amazing man of God who possesses an integrity unrivaled by most other men I know.

His strength of conviction and depth of faith were put on

public display the last three years as he cared for and loved his wife Kristen while she battled terminal cancer. She passed away in January 2014, yet Kurt has diligently and faithfully loved his four children, his new son-in-law, and our church from his new role as the leader of Further Still Ministries.

I was blessed to become Kurt's friend along the way. I spent a fair share of time volunteering in our Men's ministry, and as such, was able to witness Kurt's heart for men, his faithfulness to his wife and his passion for his family. He is one of my earthly role models across various dimensions of manhood.

One key reason I found myself serving in his ministry was the downstream effect of his ability to shoulder tap other men to serve. See, Kurt had recruited my brother-in-law, Jeff Heisler, among his core leadership team. Within this inner circle of godly men, Kurt not only asked them to serve in various capacities, he taught them how to approach other men to do the same. My shoulder tap came one Saturday morning as my wife and I hosted a yard sale.

Jeff and his family had stopped by our annual front yard extravaganza. We were not exactly deluged with crowds, so there was plenty of down time. During one of the lulls, Jeff and I chatted about various topics. He said, "You know what, Kent, you'd make a great volunteer for an event at church. Have you heard about the Valentine's banquet we host each year for married couples?"

It was an innocent enough discussion, but this single interchange had a profound effect on my life. I jumped into the planning for that event, and as we progressed, I discovered that I had some aptitude for event planning, volunteer engagement, and project management. That role led me to another, leading our annual men's fall retreat. At a large church, events like these draw hundreds of attendees, so managing the planning and execution of the event was not a trivial exercise. As a result of these and other subsequent roles, I became a better leader, motivator, and communicator. Undoubtedly, I still have much to learn, but the series of increasingly challenging volunteer commitments accelerated my development.

Jeff shoulder-tapped me and specifically asked me to engage: one-on-one and with a direct connection to both an area of passion for me (marriage) and in an area where I had some skill and potential for more (event management). Jeff did not ask me to handle finances or to address bigger men's ministry strategic topics. At that point in my life, I was not ready for either. But planning an event? I knew I could handle that, have some fun with it, and live to tell the tale.

As I peeled back the onion over time, I realized that Jeff had been modeling Kurt Sauder's behavior and approach. Kurt is a master at discovering the skills and passions of other men and then calling them to step up and use those skills for the kingdom. Notice that there are two parts to this equation: the discovery (shoulder-spotting) and the call (shoulder-tapping).

You may wonder why you struggle to engage other men. You may be leading a church or committee that is perpetually under-resourced and you long for the day when able men will step into key roles. Or maybe you're the boss at a company in which the employees do their job to the letter of the law, but never stretch beyond to contribute in other areas. You desire more committed team members or a deeper resource pool, but there seems to be a shortage of able-bodied and willing people to serve.

Could it be you're missing the first ingredient in this shoulder-tapping recipe—the power of observation?

See, observation is not fast, cheap, or easy. It requires you to invest time and have an open mind regarding the gifts and passions of others. Often we have a need in mind and try to find those skills in the people around us. Our eyes and ears play tricks on us and we see "skills" that are not really present, simply because our need is great. Effective observation requires we honestly assess the skills and passions of those around us and not try to implant certain capabilities just through the power of positive thinking.

Maybe you've been in this spot. Let's say your church needs more help in the parking lot, but your volunteer base? Slim pickings.

So you nab your consummate people-person. He's fun to ask because he's a fun guy—loves a crowd, loved by the crowd. You ask him to oversee directing traffic after services on Sunday. However, his skills are not a great fit, and before you know it, he's on the hook for one fender bender and two parking lot shouting matches one Sunday. Then it hits you: you needed a safety-conscious hardliner, not Mr. Talksalot, who was too busy waving at people to understand the meaning of his hand signals. You failed the observation section of the test.

We figure one size fits all when enlisting volunteers, and this is understandable. Sometimes you need to fill a gap quickly and people have to step into roles they are not perfectly suited toward. However, it's not a good long-term strategy. If some event is important enough to need you as a people-finder, it's important enough to find the right sorts of people.

Kurt wouldn't make that mistake. What makes him such an effective leader of men is not his mouth, but his ears, heart, and eyes. He listens with intent. He feels with passion. He sees unobstructed. "Ears that hear and eyes that see—the LORD has made them both" (Proverbs 20:12). Because Kurt was so gifted at this, over time, he found himself surrounded by talent, which he would readily admit was superior to his own in many ways. They say, "If you want something done right, you have to do it yourself." You know what I'm figuring out about "they"? Sometimes "they" couldn't be more wrong!

If Kurt had tried to do it all himself, we'd have a mess instead of mastery. Instead, on his core leadership team, Kurt had accomplished engineers, financial wizards, construction professionals, successful entrepreneurs, and caring shepherds. His level of volunteer engagement and leadership was exceptional, and I credit this to his ability to honestly seek out those who had the hands and heart he needed to fill roles along the way.

I don't believe this power of observation is half the equation. I think it's more like 80 percent of it. Once you can see the man emerging, calling him to engage becomes a simpler matter.

Kurt loves to hunt, so I will use a hunting analogy. Before I do, a caveat. In the end, the would-be volunteer is not felled by a single shot, dragged across two hundred yards of brush and bled dry while hanging from a sturdy branch. Now, you may have volunteers on whom you want to try that, but I don't recommend it. It's bad for recruiting.

Kurt was a skilled hunter of men. He could observe you from a distance and get close before you sensed his presence.

By the time you saw him, the arrow was already flying. Resistance was futile. You were ensnared!

The key difference: Kurt was not taking your life, but he was giving you a chance to willingly surrender it. And we have a model for that. Jesus found people in all walks of life, observed them, and tapped them on the shoulder. "Follow me," he said. And we never read about people saying, "Well, I guess; I kind of wanted to take a year off from committees." No, they were captivated by the opportunity they saw as he embodied it. They were willing to give something up to get something better. People knew Jesus looked at them and saw eternal worth.

Similarly, if you found yourself in Kurt's sights, it was because you were a trophy possession. But not for him—for the Lord.

Therefore, when the "call" came, you were already inclined to accept it. Normally, this came over a cup of coffee or a sandwich at a local deli (or at your yard sale). Kurt, or one of his trained fellow assassins like my brother-in-law, would make an observation about you ("Hey, you seem to enjoy working with numbers."). That's when you knew the fix was in, though you also discovered you didn't mind at all.

Because then he would connect your gifts to the church's needs: "Boy, do we need someone who can do what you do!" Then he'd ask you to jump in: "Would you consider helping us out?"

As any good hunter knows, observing the patterns of the animal is a key determiner of success. One might have great aim, but if he lacks an understanding of the prey's behavior, he will have nothing on which to set his sights.

LESSONS LEARNED

This is what set Kurt apart and it's what can make us much more effective in recruiting and retaining talent, be that in volunteer or paid positions. We can't settle for a warm body in a role that doesn't suit the individual. At best we'll get temporary relief, but no long-term cure. At worst, we put someone in a position to fail, undermining our efforts as well as destroying their confidence.

Most of us need to learn this simple pattern in recruiting:

1) Identify: see the problem or need.
2) Create: envision a solution, maybe with wise counsel.
3) Scope: Scope out the resources required.
4) Pray: Ask God to bring the resources/people.
5) Observe: Rightly notice when they show up.
6) Ask: Personally ask someone to help.

Many executives and ministry professionals give into the temptation to focus only on Step 1 and Step 6—skipping all those in between. "Hey, we need a traffic guy for next weekend. Just grab somebody!" This leads to shallow resource pools, frustrated teams, and incomplete missions.

Finally, each of us needs to accept our role in the process. Often, we simply do what we have been asked to do. We dodge and hide as long as we possibly can, and, when we finally lose the game of "Tag, You're It," we give in. We need to look at our participation in a new way, and even shoot for involvement at a higher level. Nearly every time, what we expect to be drudgery turns out to be a blessing we never anticipated. Great stuff happens while we're on duty rather than sitting in the recliner watching yet another game. And when we dodge those opportunities, we're dodging the richest blessings of God.

Finally, we need to be co-recruiters (like my brother-in-law) and co-identifiers of talent. Quite often we have a far superior vantage point to the gifts of the people around us, as compared to the pastor or leadership team. We need to be resident talent scouts, always with a mind toward helping to make the church or organization healthier by unearthing gifts no one knew about, to invest toward needs everyone sees.

Questions to Consider

• *Are you answering the call of your leaders and filling a role in your organization?*

• *Should you be more engaged in the process of identifying and recruiting talent?*

• *Think of five people you personally know who aren't fully engaged in the organization's missionWhat are their talents? What do they enjoy doing? If you don't know, set out to watch and learn. Ask God to help you find the gifts of others this week.*

• *Do you have someone in a role today for which they are not well suited? Do you need to offer them a get-out-of-jail-free card and allow them to step down?*

15

COMMAND CALMLY

Be a Man of Few(er) Words

I'm an extrovert. I can be loud and boisterous at times. Perhaps I suffer from Short Man's Disease.

If I do, I come by it honestly. You could lay a plank across the heads of my mother, father and three siblings and it would be roughly five feet three inches off the ground, and perfectly level to the ground. I may, at times, use my big mouth and loud laugh to get attention and be noticed. Just call me Little Big Mouth. It's who I am, okay?

On one hand, it's the way I'm wired, and I don't believe I'll ever become a soft-spoken intellectual with elbow pads on my sweaters and a pipe in my mouth, rocking slowly in my library. On the other hand, this can reveal an insecurity and a lack of humility.

C. S. Lewis wrote in Mere Christianity that when we meet truly humble people, we never come away noticing their humility. We haven't heard them talking themselves down, because only the self-obsessed spend time doing that. What we'd remember is how captivated by us they were. Lewis concludes that the essence of biblical humility isn't thinking less of ourselves, but thinking of ourselves . . . less.

This is why I'm awestruck by the men in my life who are quiet or soft spoken, yet have tremendous leadership capacity. They are humble men, genuinely interested in others, and they don't have to be loud or boisterous to command attention.

One of these men I've observed up close is Brad DeVries. Brad is a Christ-follower. He is a loving but firm father, a fiercely devoted husband, a former Marine Corps pilot, and an experienced and thoughtful real estate CEO. He has served as the Chairman of our church elder board.

The best part: Brad would shrug off most of this, just acknowledging that he has been blessed, redeemed and to his own surprise, used by God to be a rock in our community. And he means it. He's the real article.

As you can imagine, I have a love-hate relationship with this man. I love all those cool things about him and how freely he has given me his time, encouragement, and support.

But!

I hate how he can do all this without ever raising his voice. I mean, he is my own personal Tony Dungy—completely under control, never hollering, yet commanding respect as a strong leader. How does he do it?

Me? I'd rather lead from my own self-confidence and communicative ability. My preference is to raise the volume control to 10, then break it off trying to make it 11.

But Brad could lead a team of high caliber men while standing in a library. I'd need to be in the middle of Chuck E. Cheese's.

Some of us men fall back on our own approaches and past patterns, without recognizing the power of a new and different method. Many of us become frozen in our high school or college-age peer influence methods, and we never move beyond that to recognize and adopt superior leadership methods.

Am I suggesting all men should become quiet leaders?

Well, yes and no. We don't want to completely fight against our giftedness. However, most often, loud leaders are merely compensating for an insecurity. It's not their volume that needs adjusting, but their self-focus.

I had the privilege of taking an intensive communication course from an accomplished trainer of public speakers, Charles Reilly. He had helped hundreds of senators, media pros, and CEOs all learn how to be more effective up front.

During his course, we would make a presentation in front of the dozen attendees and then Charles would give feedback.

After one of my talks he said, "Kent, you talk really fast."

I quickly admitted, "Yes, I know I need to slow down."

He stepped closer to me with palms up, "No! Don't slow down. Just pause more often."

He went on to say that trying to slow me down would be like trying to get a sports car to plow through mud (his analogy, not mine). It was important to be true to myself. However, I needed to pause more often to allow the audience to process what I was saying and mentally catch up to where I was in the flow of thought.

Great advice. He saw my strength and found a way to leverage it fully without stripping me of my personality.

I don't want to suggest that gregarious and fun-loving individuals try to remove all passion from their personal toolkit. Yet passion doesn't have to manifest itself in verbal dominance. Passion doesn't need pedal to the metal every moment.

And let's face it, do we see ourselves surrounded by leaders who are "too quiet" or "too accommodating" of others? Quite the opposite! If our leadership pendulum needs to swing, for most of us, it needs to head toward a more deferential and inclusive approach.

I recall a lunch with Brad that was super painful, very quiet—yet life-giving and powerful. I had acted foolishly and shared my struggle with Brad to get his perspective. He was kind and accommodating. But neither did he mince words.

During our lunch he said things like, "Well, this is an area that I have become ruthlessly aggressive in trying to prevent in my life," and, "If you need to switch jobs to keep this from happening, it would be worth it." Powerful concepts—but he laid it all on me gently.

He was emphatic, deliberate, aggressive but not loud. In fact, he even seemed to get quieter the longer we were together. Rather than increasing the level of anxiety, he reduced it through his demeanor.

I wanted one of those t-shirts that said:

KEEP CALM AND LISTEN TO BRAD

Men, we must learn this skill. For many reasons.

First, this helps others feel secure with us. Brad and I were in a public place, but I knew that our conversation was private. Heads were not turning in surprise to hear Brad giving me the what-for. A quiet tone conveys trust and sincerity. It keeps us calm. It opens the door for others to be more open with us.

Second, it helps us actually be heard. It may seem counter-intuitive, but the quieter we are, the more people tend to lean in. If you're old enough, you remember the E. F. Hutton ads (You hipsters stop the brow-wrinkling and Google it). One reason our wives and children don't listen to us is due to our aggression and loudness. We need to be a pleasant fountain, not a pounding firehose (or a babbling brook).

Third, this helps others parse our words more effectively. If someone is always hollering, then how do we know which elements are more important than others? When we communicate in a kind and gentle manner, it only takes a pinch of seasoning to highlight a key point. That which is constantly shouted becomes white noise.

Fourth, it helps keep our own ears open. You have heard it said that God gave us two eyes, two ears, and only one mouth for a reason. (Also, three eyes or two mouths or just about anything else just looks weird.)

Four inputs, one output. When our tone goes down, our antenna goes up. We hear better when we adopt a calm posture.

As with all things related to true manhood, our model is Jesus Christ. On this topic of quiet command, where does He fall? Well, we do see him being emphatic many times in scripture—with the Pharisees in particular. We also see aggression and righteous anger with regard to the money lenders in the temple.

However, the vast majority of his recorded dialogue seems to be delivered in a conversational tone. He may have spoken up so that listeners could hear, but, we don't see him ranting and hollering, especially not when talking with believers or those he was hoping would believe. This is our key observation. Do we speak with the tone and volume of Christ?

When we try to use volume to be heard, we're using the world's methods. Consider for a moment the talk shows on television, the movies at the theater, and the music on our iPods. Those who want to be heard in this world must become increasingly loud, edgy, and shocking. The crazier and more alarming, the more followers on Twitter.

Yet I'd argue that is not the model we see in Scripture. Take the apostle Paul for example. If he were alive today, he might be inspired to send his message to churches using videos instead of ink on parchment. Think about that for a moment. What would be the vibe on Paul's YouTube Channel? Can you see Paul screaming on the video like Jim Cramer doling out the latest stock tip? Would Paul be hollering at Timothy or red faced and screaming, "Foolish Galatians, who has bewitched you?" I don't think so.

Now, could we see Paul dropping an occasional line such as, "I can do all things through Christ who gives me strength," as an impassioned plea, a call to arms like Mel Gibson in Braveheart? Perhaps. There are certainly some moments that Paul might have wanted to highlight, and he may have taken it up a notch to make his point.

Even so, I don't think that would have been his dominant style. It's hard to convey love with an elevated tone and a raised fist. Paul's intention was to become all things to all men so that he might win some. Hmm, "win some" sounds a lot like "winsome". I don't know about you, but having someone yell at me is not very winsome. It's kind of lose-some, actually.

Let's commit to retaining our passion and conviction, but wrapping it with winsome deference through a tone of quiet command. We don't need to be the loudest voice in the room to have the most influence. We will not let our own insecurities drive us to a high-pitched approach.

I'm grateful to Brad for so effectively modeling this approach to me. He is a modern-day example of a man who loves others so much that he gently delivers his perspective.

Questions to Consider

• *When you don't feel like you're being heard, do you raise your voice?*

• *Would people describe you as loud and boisterous? Is that possibly connected to an insecure need to be the life of every party?*

• *How can you use this approach to be more effective? Would it help you in your leadership role to occasionally turn the volume way down in order to make an emphatic point?*

SIGN UP. PITCH IN.

Grow Through Volunteering

I have many mental images of my dad, Stan Evans, from my childhood. Two snapshots are most indelibly seared into my memory banks.

First, there's the picture of him underneath one of our family cars. He was a salesman during the week and a master mechanic on weekends. I handed him many a quarter-inch ratchet and flathead screwdriver. I also learned that evidently cars had ears but poor hearing. Otherwise, why did he holler at them so often?

Second, there's the picture of him in his coaching shirt at the baseball field. And, this one isn't only in my mind—it's in my basement. In a shoebox. I love the photo: his shirt had his name stitched in cursive, Stan Evans, Coach, Executive Board.

That last part is the topic of this chapter. My father was not only a parent of players and a volunteer coach. Along with a group of other men, he had helped form the sports league where I spent the vast majority of my waking hours from birth to age 18. In watching him pour his time and energy into this sports league, I subconsciously learned the importance of volunteering.

As a small child, I thought our baseball league "just happened." Fields were marked with white chalk, umpires showed up, baseballs were in buckets and bats hung on the fence. They just did that themselves. I never noticed the work behind the scenes required to pull all this off. As I grew older, I realized that men like my dad were the guys who raked and watered the fields, scheduled people to work in the concessions, and hired (and fired!) the umpires.

When I played there, Beechmont Youth Baseball had three fields. The largest one we cleverly called "the big field." You advanced to this monster when you turned 14. The left field fence measured out at 310 feet, but it might as well have been a thousand. I never hit a home run there, and only came close once or twice. The fence and the plate were in different zip codes.

The giant power distribution box controlling the lighting was out behind that left field fence. Beyond that, bordering the ballpark, there was an apartment complex. The ballpark wasn't situated in the richest neighborhood of our town, so the apartments seemed mysterious and even a little spooky.

At the end of a long summer's night of baseball, my dad was often the last guy at the park, so he was responsible for turning out the lights. I accompanied him dozens of times to the scary abyss behind the left field wall. He had a ring of keys. He'd snag one that opened the padlock on the lighting control system and throw open the big metal doors.

Inside the box, the on/off switch was one of those giant handles affixed to the side of an electrical panel. He'd yank the switch and instantly we were engulfed by darkness. As our eyes adjusted to the pitch black, he'd close the panel doors, snap the padlock shut, and we'd make the 400-foot walk back to civilization.

Somewhere along those walks in the dark, I realized something. My dad basically ran this place. Things like concessions and tryouts and double-elimination tournaments did not magically manifest themselves. He made it happen. My dad was a critical cog in the Beechmont Baseball machine. He had the embroidered shirt to prove it. He was a volunteer.

This realization progressively dawned on me as I hit my teenage years. Eventually he let me take his keys and head out to flip the switch all by myself. The foot speed I needed to make my competitive high school soccer team was enhanced by the many sprints I made from the dark panel box back to safety!

Beyond left field was scary enough. But scary plus dark plus no dad brought out the world-class sprinter in me. I just knew that Freddy Krueger lived in those apartments.

When I turned 16, I snagged a paying job at the ballpark. I'll go out on a limb and speculate that my dad's role on the board had something to do with that. As the summer field maintenance man, I was old enough to drive the small tractor we used to drag the fields. I proudly clutched my own personal keys to the kingdom of baseball. Sadly, my tenure was short lived.

One hot summer day as I drug the field, I became too focused on watching the chain-link drag behind me. This was a necessary task to be sure the drag did not catch itself in the fence—I'd watched my dad handle it. But if you watched too long, you steered off course. That's precisely what happened as I plowed into the first base dugout on the "middle" field.

I severely bent the posts holding up the dugout roof and damaged the fence badly. That was a rough night at the park, as I was now infamous. People were whispering to each other behind their popcorn, "Psssst—it was Stan Evans' kid who did that! Yessir, he smashed up the place with the tractor, that one."

With a blackened name, I was demoted to the lowest rung of the baseball world. Yes, I became an umpire, a role which did not require the operation of heavy machinery. Or keeping an eye on anything.

I was learning life lessons; I just didn't realize it. At the time, it felt more like just wrecking stuff. But in retrospect, on those hot and dusty fields, I discovered how to pour myself into something just for the love of the organization. I learned that many of the things that we take for granted—sports leagues, youth groups, scouting troops—don't happen on their own. They require the diligent and selfless service of men and women who bring their talents and skills to bear for the benefit of others.

Speaking of talents, my dad was always quick with numbers. His high math aptitude was routinely put on display. When I went to buy my first car, we were talking with a salesperson who was clearly outmatched in math dueling. As my dad negotiated, the hapless salesman would turn to his calculator to figure up the financial impact of various tweaks to the deal. Before he could even finish punching in the numbers, my dad would blurt out, "The new payment will be $138 per month."

The sales guy would put on that "we'll just see about that" grin, only to frown 15 seconds later as he realized my dad could beat up his calculator.

It was no surprise to me. My dad had demonstrating his

processing power in the sports arena. He established league fees, developed budgets, negotiated purchases, and created compensation plans for umpires (thanks for that last one, Pops!). He has also given me financial tips and advice throughout my life. He discovered ways to take one of his personal and career strengths and put it to use for the benefit of others. I've tried to model that in my life.

I was once asked by one of our church elders to take on a key role within a major capital campaign. I knew I'd be diving into the deep end, and I'd need God's guidance to keep my head above the surface. I also knew God had given me a set of unique life experiences, gifts, and talents, and the capital campaign represented an opportunity to fully leverage those for His kingdom. I jumped in.

I know a lot of guys don't like tests. They think of the algebra ordeal of days past. If that's you, you need to get over it and go take a skill inventory. Find out what you're wired to accomplish. You may not have my dad's eerie powers of multiplication and division, but surely you're good for something! My test results said, "Avoid tractors." But it turned out I could do other stuff. So can you.

We need to know our strengths and apply them in civic, personal, and nonprofit contexts. You may be an accountant by training, but on the weekends, you help direct traffic in the church parking lot. There's nothing wrong with stepping up in areas of need or stretching beyond our comfort zones. However, are you being fully utilized in a way that increases your enthusiasm for the organization? Have you ever sat down, crafted a list of your skills, then asked yourself the question, "How can I use these skills to advance the causes I'm passionate about?"

Here are just a few examples of people I've seen leverage their abilities in some volunteer capacity.

- A real estate professional helped his church negotiate facility contracts.
- A salesman leveraged his communication skills to help fathers write letters to their children.
- A business executive used his strategic planning acumen to support new church plants.
- A former contractor launched a ministry to tackle handyman projects for needy people.
- An engineer built a proactive disaster response plan for his church.

I'm grateful for a father who set a fantastic example in this area for me. Through the power of hindsight, I can look back and see how deeply influenced I was by his volunteerism. Thanks, Dad!

Questions to Consider

• *What are your talents and skills? What makes you successful at your job? Do you have a head for numbers, like my dad, or an eye for design, or an ear for music?*

• *Can you take that skill and pour it into an organization whose mission truly excites you?*

• *Who do you know who is great at doing this already? What can you learn from them?*

• *Can you bring those skills home and impact your own family?*

17

SIMPLY EXCEL

Your Map to Mastery

In the introduction—if you can remember back that far—we discussed the aim of this book. It's not just that you glean wisdom from the men I've met and the lessons they have taught me—though that's beneficial. I'd rather you learn to gather these lessons from the men around you. That's the real prize.

Imagine if enough of us guys could become human sponges, soaking up lessons in all contexts, everywhere we went. Life lesson machines! We could spawn a nice-guy revolution.

Let's recapture our ability to learn and grow from one another. It will enable us to be more effective, successful, and influential. We'll be better and more pleasant people to be around, but we'll also make the environment around us better.

In this chapter, I want to unpack the methods to my madness. I've broken them into two categories. First, we'll cover a sequence of steps you can walk through to get started. Then we'll address some key tips to help you get maximum value out of these engagements. Some of these will be obvious, even painfully so. Some are a bit more subtle.

For the obvious ones, here's my challenge for you: conduct an honest personal inventory of how effective you are at implementing the approach. It's one thing to understand, it's another to implement. Conceptually, I understand how to play guitar, but you don't want to listen to me try.

Your knee-jerk reaction may be to brush some of this off as too plain to be helpful. However, if we're honest with ourselves, we can probably find ways to increase our effectiveness or frequency. And, if you want a man-sized challenge, ask a good friend or your wife to evaluate you. Caveat emptor. (Google it. Do I have to explain everything?)

THREE STEPS YOU CAN TAKE RIGHT NOW

STEP 1: CLIMB DOWN

The foundational building block to learning from those around us is simply an acknowledgment that we have something to learn. Sounds obvious, but many of us miss this one. We must get down off our high horse and adopt a posture of humility. See, it's relatively easy to believe that Warren Buffet could teach us something about money or that Billy Graham could show us how to communicate. When we compare ourselves to the über-talented and world famous, our learning gap is obvious.

Yet how about our brother-in-law with the godly adult children? Or that subordinate at work with a penchant for physical training? Or your wife with her crazy cooking skills? Are you willing to step into someone's world, admit they know something you don't, and seek to learn?

If we can do this, then all other doors fly open for us.

STEP 2: DETERMINE GAPS

Armed with the realization that you have some room to grow, you can now identify the gaps you would most like help in closing. You may figure out that you want to become a better parent, boss, communicator, or project manager. It's difficult to find answers if we don't know the questions. Knowing the areas in your life you'd like to further develop enables you to start finding those who can help you.

If you're struggling to find specific areas where you can improve, this is where a trusted, honest friend comes in handy.

For me, my best friend in this area is my wife. She's not a nag or critic, but she's always willing to give me an honest assessment of where and how I can grow. I also have a few other friends who will point out areas that need strengthening. These truth-tellers are key assets in my life.

STEP 3: SPOT HELPERS

Now we begin the hunt. We know we need help and we have a few specific areas or topics in mind. Remember those tests in grade school where we had to match the words on the leftwith the corresponding definitions on the right? That's where we are in the process. We now start matching our areas of growth with people around us. These might be people we already know or those we'll soon meet.

It's amazing how quickly God tends to bring us help when we realize we need it. You may decide that you want to learn piano on a Monday and at your child's play on Tuesday you sit next to a virtuoso pianist. When we have our antenna up, it's almost comical how quickly someone steps into our life who can help.

Now that we're identifying our helpers, let's talk about how we can be highly effective in learning from them.

11 TIPS TO HELP YOU BE A WISE GUY HUNTER

TIP #1: BE SINCERE

As we approach others for help, we must be sincere. We cannot have some other angle.

Several years ago I was connecting one gentleman (Matt) who had a high degree of financial experience with another friend (Joe) who was running a small nonprofit. When I called Matt to set up the appointment, he surprisingly asked, "You guys looking for money?"

I shot back, "How long have you and I known each other?" He figured it had been more than a decade. I continued, "How often have I asked you for money?" He thought for a second then acknowledged I had never called seeking donations—despite his obvious capacity to give them.

I concluded, "Super. So let's agree that if I ever do want your money, I'll begin the conversation asking for it! No sir, I just need you to give this guy 30 minutes of accounting advice." We both chuckled and set up the meeting.

I had earned the right to push back with him because I had been sincere in our previous dealings. While this gentleman has unusual financial resources, I had never tried to tap them and had therefore earned his trust.

Ironically, at the writing of this book, I'm leaning on him pretty hard to support a different nonprofit! But at least he knows when I ask for something that is the thing I truly want, and I'm not just trying to get close enough to snatch his wallet. Successful people sometimes become suspicious of those who approach them, smelling insincerity even when it's not there. Be sincere to earn trust.

TIP #2: AVOID FLATTERY

I recommend the following sentences, especially if you don't know an individual particularly well.

Joe, you have a lot of experience in (insert field here), and I'd like to learn a few things about that. Could I possibly buy you a cup of coffee and pick your brain?

That's it. Simple and straightforward.

We can be tempted to think that to approach a skilled and talented individual, we must have first memorized their résumé and be able to spit it back to them. "You're so incredible, may I come and collect the crumbs at your feet? I promise to not interfere with your aura of greatness."

Get real. Most guys, even those who have attained proficiency or prominence in their field, can clearly recall what it felt like to learn the ropes. They don't need to be propped up with flattery. It's a turn-off. Not that I discourage you from saying any of those things to me. I especially like hearing about my aura of greatness. Just an FYI.

TIP #3: DO YOUR HOMEWORK

I interviewed a young man a few years ago for a role in my employer's company. He kept asking me basic questions about our company—stuff he could have discerned in a 15-minute review of our website. It grated on me so badly I finally had to level with him, "Billy, listen—if you were interviewing for this role 15 years ago, I could understand how finding this information might have been difficult. However, in today's wired world, you're merely demonstrating that you haven't done your homework on us at all."

With Google searches and social media tools aplenty, we can often get at least a rudimentary dossier on an individual, even someone we have never met. Clearly, there's a fine line between coming across as interested in them and being a creepy stalker, so be careful. However, in an opening cup of coffee, one comment can go a long way, such as, "I noticed that you're on the board of ABC organization. Do you mind telling me how you became involved there?"

That's much better than, "I noticed your family's vacation last month on Facebook. How was that cookout on the beach?" Yikes!

TIP #4: AVOID SELF DEPRECATION

Yes, you're seeking their expertise. Yes, they may be more financially successful or have a better marriage or be quite accomplished on the pan flute. But you still have a pulse and a right to exist. It's not winsome but worrisome to approach skilled men by asserting how useless and incomplete you are. "It's just your world and I'm sorry for taking up space in it." As we discussed earlier, overdoing it with self-deprecation is simply "Me, me, me" to a different tune.

I recall attending a meeting with about 30 men. We were discussing ideas for how the group could move forward. One gentleman spoke up and, in the span of five minutes, told us no fewer than four times how underqualified he was to be speaking up. "I know I'm not perfect in this area. I'm just opening my big mouth. There are others more qualified for sure." It was frustrating, because between the sad disclaimers, he was actually proposing a worthwhile idea. He came across not as humble, but as self-focused, which only seemed to cloud his solid ideas.

TIP #5: BE DIRECT

Just last week I was contacted by an acquaintance. I know this person and like him, though we're not close friends. We might bump into each other socially once a year and exchange pleasantries. He's a good dude, just not in my inner circle. He opened our call with 15 minutes of "catching up." Then, finally, he got to the point, which was to ask me for a small favor.

I didn't mind the favor. In fact, I agreed to help. However, if he were asking my advice, I'd have suggested he invert the order of the discussion. It would have seemed more natural and appropriate if he had opened with, "Hey Kent, I'm calling to ask a favor." Then, after getting that out of the way, we could have enjoyed catching up.

When contacting someone for advice or help, be direct. State at the onset the reason you're calling. Then, after you either get the advice you need or set up the appointment, take a minute (or 10) to catch up, depending on your relationship with the individual. If you lead with pleasantries, it can come across as a disingenuous set up.

TIP #6: BE "ALWAYS ON"

Sometimes we identify an individual with skill in an area and we chase them down to learn more about that specific thing. However, many of our greatest learnings come simply from being open to learning. If you browse back through the stories in this book, you'll find some came from men who I sought out and knew I could learn from. But much of my learning caught me by surprise, coming to me through chance encounters or observations I wasn't looking for at the moment.

For example, I was in London, expecting to learn about nonprofit management from Mr. Parsons. I did. However, I also learned about having a perpetual posture of prayer and humility, how to encourage a brother, and how to speak truth in love. I expected to learn how to run a lighting division from Frank Austin, but along the way, I learned how to ask great questions and how to increase my influence. We trip across many hidden and serendipitous finds along our journey, if we're open to them.

TIP #7: BE REFERRED

Obviously, it's much easier to connect with someone when you're introduced by a mutual friend. Allow me to provide one nuanced tip that can help you increase your referrals: specificity. When you approach your circle of acquaintances, be as specific as you can be regarding what you're after. It might seem counterintuitive, but the tighter you focus your request, the more quickly someone can find you a connection.

I'm routinely contacted by folks in job transitions. "Hey," they think, "that Kent guy knows all about being out of work. He's a guru of unemployment—I think I'll ask him."

They may be looking for specific openings or just to network in a new industry. One guy asked me, "What companies do you know who are hiring?"

I asked for more specifics, but he couldn't give them—he just needed a job. I desperately wanted to help, but it's hard to paint a masterpiece with a broad brush. Contrast that with another friend who once asked, "Who do you know in the medical device arena?"

Bam. Connection made, he was hired a few months later.

TIP #8: SHUT YER TRAP

There are two foundational truths in interpersonal communications.

1) Asking is steering: If you're the person asking the questions, you're usually the one charting the course of the conversation.

2) Listening is learning: If you're doing most of the

listening, then, you're usually doing most of the learning. We talk to teach; we listen to learn.

It's been a tough lesson for me to learn. My closest friends might argue I still have a long way to go in the craft of listening, but what are they arguing about that for? I thought they were my closest friends. Never mind.

The power of simply listening and letting others talk has been a game-changer for me. I try to gently steer a conversation through intentional questions and then sit back and receive. It's not easy for me. I love to communicate and share my ideas. However, if I'm to be an effective learner, I must become a better listener.

Great musicians train their brains to hear the metronome even when it's not there. Likewise, when we're in learning mode, we need our brain to be tracking our talk time vs. the other person's. To maximize our learning, that ratio should be at least 40/60. We should talk 40 percent of the time and listen 60. If it tilts more to the other person, they may be heading down paths we don't find as valuable. If it tilts more toward us, we're squandering the opportunity to tap their wisdom.

TIP #9: PRAY FIRST

As noted in Tip #6, we can't always know when someone

is about to teach us something. There is no notification e-mail or "coming attractions" trailer. Lessons like to jump out and surprise us; they're goofy that way.

However, there are many times when we're connecting with an individual for the specific purpose of picking their brain on some topic. In those cases, it's immensely helpful to pray before the encounter.

I find that praying before meeting with someone helps me fully open myself to learning during our encounter. My heart softens, putting me in a humbler position. I'm ready to receive. My ears open wider allowing me to pick up on subtle cues during our conversation, telling me what to ask next or what topics to avoid. Even my body posture can become more deferential and nonthreatening. Praying is like priming the pump—it gets my learning juices flowing.

TIP #10: BECOME LESS DEFENSIVE

I worked closely with Mark, a man I highly respected. We had two interactions, within the span of two working days, that moved in different directions. On a Friday, we disagreed on something, but our exchange was respectful, professional, and in the end we resolved the issue. On the following Monday, our discussion on a different topic was laced with frustration, and after hollering at one another we retreated to our separate corners. We had resolved nothing.

I trusted this man, so on Tuesday I called him up and I asked for a few minutes to debrief. When we sat down, I said, "Mark, on Friday we had a respectful exchange. On Monday, not so much. You said on Monday that I was 'very defensive.' I want to walk the line between being an ardent defender of my position and being a defensive individual. I want to excel at the former and never be the latter. What was the difference between my approach on Friday versus Monday?"

He went on to tell me several things that were not particularly easy to hear, though I knew they were true. He helped me see that when I became defensive, it caused everyone's walls to go up. People would become less likely to cooperate with me. It was a beneficial exchange for me.

If you're to become a great learner from other men, you must lose the defensive posture. You can ardently defend your ideas, but be open to input from others. Remember, the heart of the personal change game is going from doing it one way, to doing it another way. That often means we must admit that our first method was not the best.

TIP #11: HONOR SENIORITY

The final tip comes from a slightly different angle: find you some old dudes and hang out.

As I noted in the chapter on Butch Dabney, there's almost no replacement for securing advice and input from men who are 10, 15, or 50 years our senior. Just the sheer number of experiences is a rich well to draw from. They are seasoned veterans at the game of life and have seen things you and I have not. They have different cultural contexts and a unique perspective on events, people and ideas.

Not to mention that as people age, society has a tendency to marginalize them. We send the signal that if they are no longer as physically adroit as they once were, then they must be less useful. This is not as true in other cultures where there is reverence for the elderly.

I once heard a woman from Africa speak. She was fielding questions from teenagers in the audience. One of the questions was about her age, and the moderator was embarrassed. He told her she needn't answer such an "impolite" question. Yet she smiled and said, "I'm glad to say that I'm 58. In our society, the older you are, the more respected you are!"

Let's do ourselves and our society a benefit by reclaiming the honor of the aged.

[1] http://www.fatherhood.org/father-absence-statistics Accessed October 24, 2015

[2] http://www.si.com/nba/point-forward/2014/02/20/lebron-james-letter-to-absent-father-miami-heat Accessed October 24, 2015

EPILOGUE

Reconnecting with Weldon

My whole journey of growth through learning began with a wise counselor named Weldon Fuller. Yet we met only a handful of times in my late teens, after which we never spoke. I had no annual checkup from the neck up, nor did I even reach out to him for the occasional cup of coffee.

What's wrong with that picture?

God knew, and he cleverly reconnected us about 25 years later.

One of my sisters took a job with the University of Louisville. One day, she and I were talking and she asked, "Hey Kent, do you recall the name of that counselor we had when we were younger? The one we met through mom's job?"

"Sure," I said, "It was Weldon Fuller." I had surprised even myself with the quick recall. It had been more than two decades since I'd seen the man, but his name never left. I'm amazed at the workings of our minds—some things stick for decades, while others slip through the mental back door five seconds after they enter. We remember mounds of trivia, but sometimes the mind seizes on something we know deep down is important. This was a name my brain wouldn't discard even after two and a half decades.

My sister continued, "Yeah, that's him! Well, I think I work with his wife. We have a lady in our office whose last name is Fuller. And her husband works as a counselor."

Naturally I was all over that one, so my sister agreed to follow up. We agreed that if her co-worker did turn out to be Weldon's wife, she would try and snag his e-mail address for me. It all happened. I was elated to once again have a link to someone who had so significantly impacted the person I'd become. I quickly punched out a note to him.

In the e-mail, I tried my best to thank him. I gave him some of the context of our discussion long ago, and did my best to give some idea of the impact he'd made on my life. I mentioned that I'd become a Christian, found an amazing, godly wife, and was raising four boys. I even told him I'd planned to write a book based on his advice: the one you're holding in your hands right now.

When my e-mail was not immediately returned, I wondered what might have happened. Maybe he hadn't received it. I realized it had become very important to me to know we'd connected and that he'd heard my gratitude.

Just as I began to reach out to my sister to confirm the e-mail, his response dropped into my inbox. I figured there could be no more fitting ending to this little book.

Thank you, Weldon.

Kent,

I've delayed responding to your special e-mail because I wanted to allow myself time to think about a meaningful response. Your thoughtfulness in writing is deeply appreciated, and I'm touched that something said all those years ago could have such impact. Although it has been a long time, I do have some remembrance of our conversation. This may be in part because of my own struggle to have a more meaningful relationship with my father. It seems you have grown greatly and have created a very meaningful life for yourself. Your idea for a book sounds terrific! Your experience and insights could be of great help to many men grappling with similar situations, and bring help to men you may never meet personally. If it works out, I'll certainly buy a copy. You mentioned having a vibrant faith in Christ and I'm delighted to know this. I deeply thank you for your kind words and for the effort to share them. For the rest, I think we might both agree—to God be the glory.

Peace and love in Christ,

Weldon

SPECIAL THANKS

CITY ON A HILL STUDIO

I would like to thank the talented professionals at City on a Hill Studio who embarked on this "Manhood Journey" with me. If I begin mentioning names, I'll leave someone out. Suffice to say that I am deeply grateful for the team's missional heart, creative chops, and cooperative spirit. It was a blessing to work on this project with you guys!

ROB SUGGS

I was blessed to work with Rob Suggs on this book manuscript. This guy is a bona fide expert and could've just shoved me around (and I'd have gladly taken it). However, he was accommodating, helpful, and generous with his time and expertise. It was an honor to work with you, sir.

MANHOOD JOURNEY

Thank you for reading about (some of) the men who came alongside me and shaped the man I am becoming. As a father, I have a sacred responsibility to mentor and love my own sons as they walk through life. I also want to surround my boys with faithful men who can support, challenge, and encourage them along their journey.

God has called me to help other fathers do this as well. He led me and several talented friends to launch an organization called Manhood Journey. This Christian non-profit helps fathers build the next generation of godly men. We provide tools and resources to help dads get fully engaged in the son-shaping process, wielding as our primary weapon God's Holy Word.

If you are a father of sons, you realize the high calling you have received. And, you also know that culture is working against us. We must seize every opportunity to build godly character in our boys. It will not happen by accident. Drop by our website to find resources that can help you intentionally build the next generation.

If you are not a father of sons, no worries! Still come on by and see how you can engage in our mission.

A. Kent Evans

Kent Evans

EMBARKING

PACK YOUR BAGS AND GO

Sample lesson from
Embarking 1 on 1
Discussion Guide

PREPARING FOR THE JOUNEY

THE BIG ROCKS

A WORD TO DAD

It is a high honor and privilege to be a dad! You are taking your responsibility seriously by being involved in this Manhood Journey with your son(s). Remember that you are not alone. Many other dads are taking this journey along with you, so depend on one another as you hike this trail. You also have a heavenly Father who is walking with you. He is your strength, your trail guide along the way. He knows this trail better than anyone because he created it.

You are embarking on a vital journey together on the trail to becoming godly men. Before meeting together with your son(s), spend some time alone with your heavenly Father. Ask him to give you the understanding, love, patience, wisdom, and words you need as you build a godly relationship with your son. Your Father has all the resources you need. Take a few moments to humbly allow him to pour everything into you that you need to be a godly dad for your son. Then you can simply overflow into your son what your Father has poured into you.

Before you begin your "meeting" with your son, ask him some open questions such as this:

What's one good thing going on at school [or on a sports team, with an interest, hobby, or activity, with your friends, etc.]?

Then just listen and ask follow-up questions.

GROUP SESSION REVIEW

Engage your son(s) in a dialogue about the meeting using any of the following questions as you see fit.

- **What did you think about our first meeting together?**
- **What was your favorite thing about it?**
- **What did you think about the illustration with the rocks?**
- **What did you learn?**
- **Did you have any questions or thoughts that you didn't have a chance to bring up (or didn't want to talk about) at the meeting?**

BE AN ACTIVE LISTENER

1. Look at your son as he speaks, keeping your body posture open and receiving.

2. Nod your head or use other nonverbal and verbal responses so he knows you're hearing him.

3. Try not to interrupt.

4. Ask follow-up questions.

5. Remember that the purpose for the questions in this guide is to initiate discussion, not give a test!

THE FIVE "BIG ROCKS"

Let's work on memorizing the Five Big Rocks.
A godly man . . .

1. **TRUSTS** God
2. **KNOWS** his Word
3. **PRAYS** fervently
4. **BUILDS** relationships
5. **SERVES** others

As with most things in life, it's important for you, Dad, to go first. That doesn't mean, however, that you must have these memorized beforehand. It means that you model the value of knowing these Big Rocks and working on this project together. Don't be surprised, in fact, if your son is able to memorize these faster than you!

There are many different memorization techniques you could use. Here are two ideas. Use whatever works best for your son.

- *Write each "Big Rock" on a literal large rock from your yard. Different sizes, colors, and shapes will aid in the memorization. Put the rocks out of sight and then pull one out and see if your son can name the "Big Rock" without seeing the words.*

- *On a page in each of your Manhood Journey Notebooks, draw a map. Think of each Rock as a stopping point along your trail. So for instance, your first stop is at "Trust God." Then make connections between that stop and the next one: In order to trust God, we need to "Know his Word," and so forth.*

Talk about what other rocks you would each add to this list. Dad, you go first. So for instance, you might add, "Takes care of his family" or "works hard." Encourage your son to tell you what he would add to these. Be sure to affirm your son's ideas; let him know you appreciate him and what he has to say. Tell him you're proud of him for what he prioritizes. Add these to your Manhood Journey Notebooks.

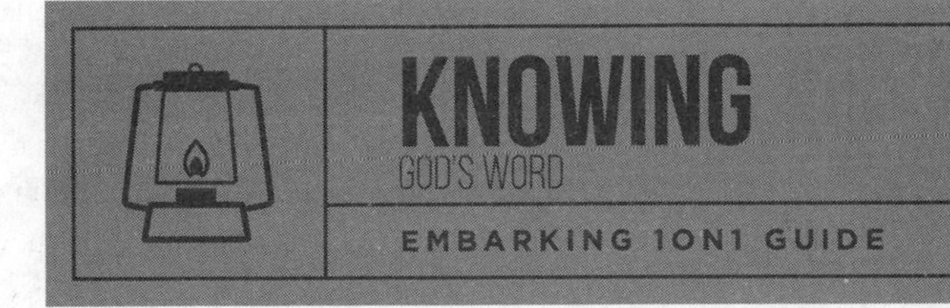

"I am the LORD your God. . . . You shall have no other gods before me."
Exodus 20:2-3

Write this verse at the top of a new page in each of your Manhood Journey Notebooks.

SAY

The very first of the Ten Commandments God gave us was that we put him first, above everything and everyone else. When we get things out of order and make other things or other people more important than God, we make those things false gods or idols. Everything else depends on putting God first in our lives, loving and trusting him.

Go over this verse several times with your son. See if your son can remember it. In future weeks you'll spend more time on memorizing the theme verse, but since you've already worked on memorizing the "Big Rocks," don't spend too much time on this here. It's far more important that you understand the vitality of putting God first in your lives than memorizing it.

The theme verse is a foundation for the rest of our Bible study. Each of the other verses we'll look at will reinforce and provide more specific ideas for how to live out the theme verse.

- Try to engage your son as much as possible in this discussion.
- As always, it's vital for you to be humble, honest, and helpful with your son.
- For each question, prayerfully decide if you should respond first or let your son initiate.
- You should share, not just ask questions. Remember, this is a dialogue!

Read or ask your son to read Matthew 22:36-40.

Which of the Five Rocks does this passage involve?

Your son may immediately say #1: Trusts God, which is right, but keep digging. Ask how the others Big Rocks relate to the passage:

- *How might "knowing God's Word" help us to love God more (especially with our minds)?*
- *How can praying fervently help us to build our relationship with God?*
- *How are Rocks 4 and 5 related to loving others as ourselves?*

Why do you think these two commands, to love God and others, are the "greatest" of all of God's commands?

Jesus was putting a priority on relationships. They are more important than money or possessions or anything else in the world. If we get these two commands right, we'll get everything else right.

If tomorrow you were to love God with all your heart, soul, mind, and strength—in other words, with everything you've got—what specifically would that look like? What would you do differently?

This is a good opportunity to honestly and humbly share an area where you find yourself struggling to love God with everything. Share only what would be helpful for your son, so that he can see that you're working on your own relationship with God. Be transparent and positive.

Read or ask your son to read Matthew 6:31-34

Background: *Jesus had been teaching the people not to worry so much about all the things they need and want in life. Instead they should trust God. Pagans are people who don't believe in God. "Righteousness" simply means living rightly for God—doing things his way, obeying him, and trusting him. Focus your discussion around verse 33.*

What comes into your mind when you think of a "kingdom"?

Your son may say a lot of things here. You might ask and discuss books or movies (i.e., The Lion King; The Princess Bride; Robin Hood; The Lion, the Witch, and the Wardrobe; The Lord of the Rings) that include kings, heroes, and battles.

If your son is young, ask him to draw a picture of what he imagines a kingdom looks like in his Manhood Journey Notebook. Then ask him questions about his picture. What's happening? Who's the hero? Who's the king? What do the subjects of a good king do?

A kingdom means there's a king!

What was Jesus saying should be our very first priority?

If God is the king and we live in his kingdom, how should we respond when he gives us a mission and directions?

EVEN DEEPER

If you would like to dig even deeper into what the Bible says about priorities, look up and discuss the following Scripture passages (it may be helpful to write these

references in your Manhood Journey Notebooks):

Isaiah 44:6
Deuteronomy 10:12-13
2 Chronicles 1:7-12
Colossians 3:1-2
1 Peter 4:7-11

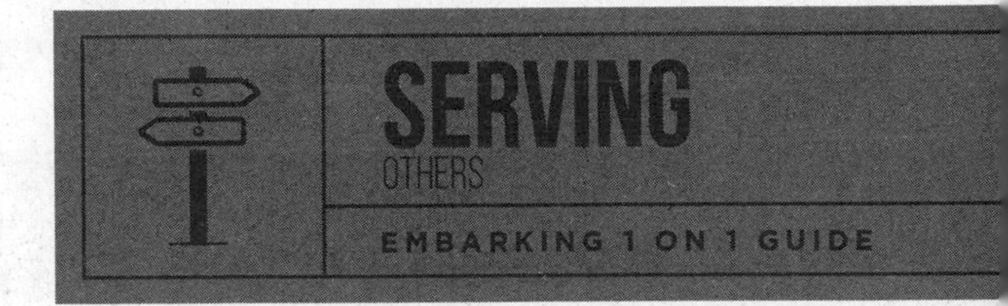

SAY

Serving others is a vital part of our journey together. When we serve others we put into action what God is doing in our lives. After all, a godly man serves others! He makes an impact on the people around him.

So let's talk about how we can make serving other people a priority in our lives. Jesus is our best example.

Read or ask your son to read Mark 10:45

How can you make it a priority this week to love and serve another person?

This can be something relatively small such as taking out the garbage without being asked, cleaning up his room, or letting his sister have first choice as to where to sit in the car, for instance. The big idea here is to simply see putting others first and serving them as a "Big Rock" in your lives, a way of trusting and obeying God.

Remember to share with your son what you will do this week to serve another person as well.

This commitment to serve others is just between you and me. It's our secret, OK? We're serving not to get the applause of others but simply to do what a godly man does.

Whatever you choose to do, write it in your own Manhood Journey Notebook.

Whatever you choose to do, write it in your own Manhood Journey Notebook.

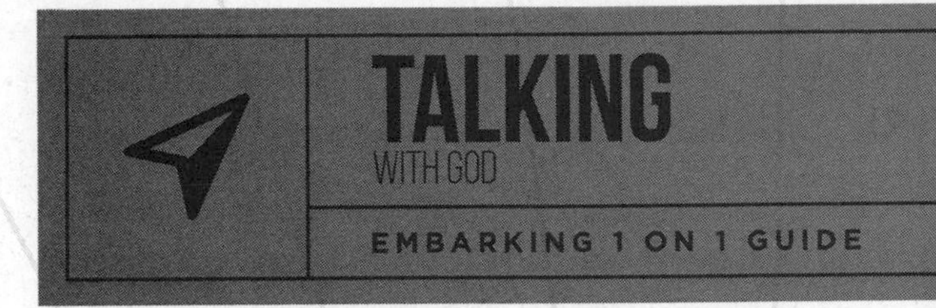

Close your time by praying for your son. Make this a very simple prayer, something such as this:

God, thanks for the time my son and I have spent together today. You know how proud I am of him and how much I love him. Please give us your strength to live for you first the rest of this week. Amen.

KENT EVANS is the board chairman and co-founder of Manhood Journey, a ministry that helps fathers and mentors build the next generation of godly men. Kent has personally experienced how the guidance of godly men can change the course of a life. Today he is blessed with a solid 20-year marriage, four wonderful sons and a fulfilling life.